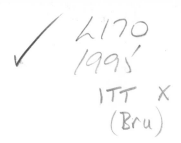
Books are to be returned on or before
the last date below.

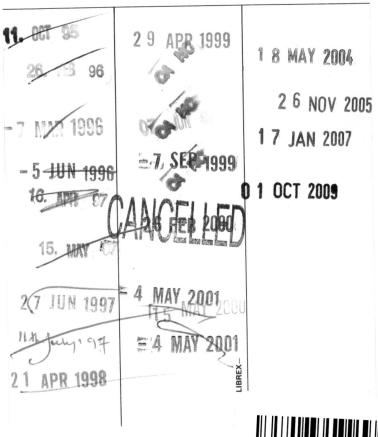

11. OCT 95   2 9 APR 1999   1 8 MAY 2004

26 FEB 96   2 6 NOV 2005

-7 MAR 1996   1 7 JAN 2007

-5 JUN 1996   -7 SEP 1999

16. APR 97   CANCELLED   0 1 OCT 2009

15. MAY 97

2 7 JUN 1997   -4 MAY 2001

11th July '97   -4 MAY 2001

21 APR 1998

LIBREX—

Symbols of the Soul
Therapy and Guidance through Fairy Tales

Books of related interest

Storymaking in Education and Therapy
Alida Gersie and Nancy King
ISBN 1 85302 519 4 hb
ISBN 1 85302 520 8 pb

Storymaking in Bereavement
Dragons Fight in the Meadow
Alida Gersie
ISBN 1 85302 176 8 pb
ISBN 1 85302 065 6 hb

Playtherapy with Abused Children
Ann Cattanach
ISBN 1 85302 193 8 hb
ISBN 1 85302 120 2 pb

Art Therapy and Dramatherapy
Masks of the Soul
Sue Jennings and Åsa Minde
ISBN 1 85302 027 hb

Chain Reaction
Children and Divorce
Ofra Ayalon and Adna Flasher
ISBN 1 85302 136 9 hb

Symbols of the Soul
Therapy and Guidance through Fairy Tales

Birgitte Brun
Ernst W. Pedersen
Marianne Runberg

Foreword by Murray Cox

Jessica Kingsley Publishers
London and Philadelphia

First published in the United Kingdom in 1993 by
Jessica Kingsley Publishers Ltd
116 Pentonville Road
London N1 9JB

Copyright © 1993 Birgitte Brun, Ernst W. Pedersen and Marianne Runberg

British Library Cataloguing in Publication Data
Brun, Birgitte
Symbols of the Soul: Therapy and Guidance
Through Fairy Tales
I. Title
615.8

ISBN: 1-85302-107-5

Printed and Bound in Great Britain by
Bookcraft Ltd., Avon

Contents

Acknowledgements

The idea to write this book, the courage and the inspiration, was given to me by Murray Cox during his supervision seminars at Gentofte Workshop in Copenhagen. He should have our thanks first of all.

Many thanks should be given to patients at Sct. Hans Hospital. They gave us their confidence. Special thanks to Paul, who also gave us permission to use his pictures. He wanted nothing in return, but expressed the wish that his story and illustrations might help other people. His name and other patients' names have been changed, of course, to provide anonymity.

Mrs Else Redknap has read the chapters by the first and the third author in order to improve our language and help us express ourselves more clearly. We are very grateful to her.

Erik Holst Ph.D. came up with new and clarifying ideas during the working process as well as much good advice. He was also very helpful when organising the manuscript.

The medical librarian Elisabeth Oxholt and the librarian Lise Simon, both from Sct. Hans Hospital, have provided us with books and articles, and have shown us literature which proved to be important in our work.

Secretary Grethe Nielsen typed materials from psychotherapy sessions with patients over many years, and followed our work with so much care and attention, also taking care of patients coming to see the psychologists. We are also grateful to secretary Anni Elsgaard for her valuable assistance.

We thank colleagues from the different disciplines. We have worked with many who shared our interest in fairy tales.

Ernst W. Pedersen wishes to thank two old friends, his nephew, sinologist Bent Nielsen, for his linguistic instinct in preparing the manuscript, and fellow hospital chaplain and psychotherapist Bent Falk for his expert perusal.

Work with fairy tales creates contact with art and science from various fields. We have found much inspiration from literature dealing with fairy tales, and we would wish that more Scandinavian books about fairy tales had been translated into English. Fortunately, the Danish expert in fairy tale interpretation Professor Bengt Holbek of the University of Copenhagen has written his comprehensive book on the subject in English. I am grateful to him for his interest in our work and valuable comments and references.

Birgitte Brun

Foreword

It is gratifying to find that a book with such a fantasy-laden title as *Symbols of the Soul* should open with a poignant vignette from the real world. Clinical records, rather than fairy tales, inform us of 'a psychotic woman who believed that she was a descendant of the Russian Tzars.... [She] wanted to be called Alexandra....' Ultimately, she drowned herself. 'She must have felt terribly lonely, never being called by the name which meant so much to her'(p.1).

This formally documented incident transpired in time and place. It was not a fairy tale of 'once upon a time', nor a fiction from 'beyond the seventh mountain'. *Symbols of the Soul* explores the interface between those two realms of discourse. More particularly, it describes and illustrates ways in which fairy tales can potentiate therapeutic endeavours. It sharpens the therapist's discernment and underlines the necessity of apposite naming.

The three authors form an interesting triad. Two clinical psychologists and a hospital chaplain are well equipped as an *ensemble*, having a trio, a tripod and the trinity at their disposal – not to mention a three-cornered hat.

The book itself has many of the best qualities of fairy tales. Its descriptive style is lucid and simple. It contains many pointers and signposts which provoke the reader's curiosity. There is transparency and verbal economy. This should not come as a surprise, when it is recalled that the authors breathe the same air as Hans Christian Andersen.

We are offered an unusual blend of experienced clinical commentary with many phrases hitherto untarnished by wear and tear. Thus we read of memory being 'refreshed'. There is also a delightfully personal account of a discussion with a taxi-driver, which leads so naturally into archetypal material and psychotherapeutic aspects of symbols.

The unthreatening capacity of fairy tales to come alongside the patients' experience, and to safely contain otherwise overwhelming affect, is clearly brought out by each contributor. There is the constant oscillation between the human predicament, such as that of the child living in custody (p.47), and the contained predicament of fairy tale custody. It is disconcerting to read (p.65) of the reduction of psychotherapeutic resources, possibly also the availability of pastoral care, however financially justified such a course of action may be. But, fortunately, the chaplain's vocation to 'administer the nurturing sacraments' (p.63) is *sui generis* and cannot be diminished. As for the sacraments themselves, they belong in another frame of reference and are certainly at home with other symbols of the soul. Such giant symbolic solidarities are immune from moth, rust and the financial axe. Sacraments and fairy tales together form a ferment of ideas and associations, a dialectic demanding discussion. There are huge theological issues about immanence and transcendence, particularity and universality, under starter's orders, waiting to be argued about.

Peter Pan – an exemplary fairy tale – is linked to the author's story (J.M. Barrie), in a way which invites further reflection upon the relationship between creativity, psychic economy and the work of art.

Pinocchio is invoked as a helper in psychotherapy. This is the only visually illustrated chapter in the book. It speaks for itself and demonstrates the energy inherent in *synaesthesia* – in which one modality 'speaks' for another. But such is the way in fairy tales.

The 'Guidance' in the sub-title is that of the imaginal, inner world. It refers to the primordial pull of the unconscious and is not to be confused with directive therapy.

This book is eclectic, lucid, simple and deep. Because it links the 'once upon a time' world with greater access to that of everyday, it is highly recommended.

Murray Cox

Introduction

Birgitte Brun

In the early 1970s I came to Sct. Hans Hospital, the oldest and largest psychiatric hospital in Scandinavia. There were then almost 2700 patients. One of the patients I met was a psychotic woman who believed that she was a descendant of the Russian Tzars. She had made an altar with candles and a table-cloth placed neatly on a small table. She had books and pictures dating from before the Russian revolution, all very colourful.

This woman, who had a strong identification with Russia, wanted to be called Alexandra, and would not accept her real Danish name. When I came to see her in the ward, I was told that she wanted to be called Alexandra, but that her wish was not to be met, since it could only confirm her in her disturbed ideas and, as staff-members, we had to stick to reality. I felt then that the professionals around her were somehow afraid that they would lose their own orientation to reality if they followed her part of the way to Russia. She had a clear sense of humour, and one day when I came to see her she said: 'Oh, there you are again with your small handbag, not knowing what on earth to do'. She was right.

One cold winter evening, Alexandra left the ward and the next morning she was found in a nearby lake. She had drowned herself. She must have felt terribly lonely, never being called by the name which meant so much to her. As professionals we were also left alone, isolated not only from the patient, but also from important aspects of our own inner world.

How could it be that dreams, fantasies, strange childhood memories and fairy tales could not bring us in contact with thoughts and feelings in this woman? Why did we deprive her of her name and disturb her very fragile identity? Why did we close our eyes and ears when confronted with a world which seemed strange to us? The answers are all part of a very long story concerning the treatment of the mentally ill in Denmark and in many other parts of the world. We will not go into the details of that story here.

Gradually, the attitude to the inner world of the psychotic patient has changed. Through psychoanalytically-oriented psychotherapy with schizophrenic patients we have achieved a better understanding. New ways of working have been used in different countries. Today, therapists from various professions apply psychotherapeutic modalities such as drama therapy, music therapy, art therapy with drawing and painting, and play therapy, and within the last decade there has been an increasing interest in the application of fairy tales as part of a psychotherapeutic process.

We hope with this book to be able to illustrate how fairy tales can be used as a support and help to children and adults, in work with emotionally deprived children, people in crisis, psychotic people or just people who are interested in fairy tales, which so many of us have lived with since we were children. The book is based on the authors' different ways of working, but also on common experiences from the same psychiatric hospital, which in 1991 celebrated its 175th anniversary (Jørgensen 1991). Two of the authors (Marianne Runberg and Birgitte Brun) are clinical psychologists; Ernst W. Pedersen is hospital chaplain. It was he who gave the book its title – *Symbols of the Soul*.

In Chapter 1, *Symbols of the Soul – Fairy Tales*, I have tried to illustrate the significance of what has been called the potential symbol. I have chosen illustrative examples from daily life and from psychotherapeutic work with psychotic patients. The significance of the potential symbol is seen in relation to

1. The instinct of self preservation.

2. The libidinal drives.

3. The intellectual drives.

4. The spiritual drives.

Chapter 2, *The Application of Fairy Tales in Psychotherapy*, deals with the description of different ways or techniques of including fairy tales in psychotherapy. Four methods have been described:

1. The naive approach.

2. The psychodynamic interpretation of fairy tales and their symbols in psychotherapy.

3. Fairy tales used as a type of play therapy.

4. Creating an individualized fairy tale as a help in personal development.

Chapter 3, *The Application of Fairy Tales in the Care and Treatment of Emotionally Deprived Children*, (by Marianne Runberg) illustrates ways in which emotionally deprived children can find healing power in fairy tales. It has to do with guidance through fairy tales, which the author differentiates from actual psychotherapy. It could be helpful to foster parents taking care of deprived children.

Chapter 4, *Fairy Tale Conversations*, is a description of the hospital chaplain's use of fairy tale conversations in a big psychiatric hospital. With patients and staff members, Ernst W. Pedersen chooses a fairy tale to read, and he is the guide when the participants talk about their associations and feelings in relation to the story. There is no limit to the topics that a patient may address. A spiritual reflection on life will often make the patients' existence more stimulating and rewarding.

Chapter 5, *Peter Pan: The Eternally Flying Child*, is a contribution to the psychoanalytically oriented interpretation of the famous figure, who has his own statue in Kensington Gardens. Looking at Peter Pan's psychological growth and development and also his developmental arrest, I have tried to draw parallels to aspects of his author J.M. Barrie's life story and to explain Peter Pan's significance in a psychotherapeutic context through a period in the treatment of a female patient with sensations of flying.

In Chapter 6, *Pinocchio as a Helper in Psychotherapy: A Case Study*, we have described in detail one of the methods we have applied, so that it should be possible to follow a developmental process. We have called it play therapy because the identification with the main figure is very close, and the actual work with the patient's problems takes place within the fairy tale world.

In Chapter 7, *The Language of Symbols in Fairy Tales*, some characteristic fairy tale symbols and possible interpretations are described – which does not mean to say that there is only one way to interpret a symbol. The symbols have been ordered in three groups.

1. Symbols of nature.

2. Magical and mythological symbols.

3. Cultural symbols.

However, organizing the symbols into groups is not of any help in the actual interpretative process. Trying to systematize the interpretative process is complicated, and will probably require a good deal of research.

Fairy tales are full of symbols, which can be understood as something very basic in our lives. They can also be seen in an individual developmental perspective. Many symbols seem to illustrate the same phenomenon, but as individuals we react differently to the symbols. Fairy tales may help us understand a person's conflicts, and they have healing power. The same fairy tale can be used with different age groups.

Bringing fairy tales into our daily work, we have felt that patients as well as staff-members responded with interest, attention and sensitivity. One of the reasons is probably that fairy tales are for all of us. They go beyond the borders of the sick and the sane, thus offering us something that it is important to share.

CHAPTER 1

Symbols of the Soul – Fairy Tales

Birgitte Brun

Symbols of the Soul

In *Archetypal Psychology* Hillman (1988, p.20) writes: 'The primary metaphor of psychology must be soul'. As he sees it, soul as metaphor describes how the soul acts, transposing meaning and releasing interior, buried significance. The relationship of the soul to death is a major theme in archetypal psychology. Hillman argues that Western culture has lost its relationship with death and the underworld, and he suggests that there is a need to re-imagine and re-animate the cultural psyche to which archetypal psychology aspires. Nyborg's concern is that knowledge of the soul of nature has been forgotten, and that this has influenced our whole attitude to life. 'Man no longer has a religious connection with nature, which results in barren intellectualism' (Nyborg 1962, p.129).

The word *archetype* comes from the Greek *archetypon*, meaning 'original'. Archetypes characterize ways of experiencing, while the instincts typify ways of acting. The archetypes form the basis of our guiding ideas. On these ideas, as explained by Jung (1956), we have founded religion, art and science. The archetypes are not in themselves visible, and it is important to emphasize their bipolar, conflicting character (see Nyborg 1962). The bipolar character could be illustrated through the maternal principle, which we find in all cultures. We meet here the positive aspect, which gives us life, and also the cruel, wicked mother, who swallows her own children, as illustrated by Birkhäuser-Oeri (1988). The archetypes create the possibilities of developing the archetypal images so essential in fairy tales.

In order to explain what analytical psychology means by an archetype, Neumann (1974) finds it important to distinguish its emotional-dynamic components, its symbolism, the material thing with which it can be compared and its structure. Working with fairy tales very much involves working with symbols, which, being related to the unconscious, are derived from archaic modes of psychic functioning. In Danish we have an illustrative word – *sindbillede*; the literal translation would be *emblem*, but really it means 'image of the mind', which is close to the symbolic attitude so essential in fairy tale reading. Cox and Theilgaard (1987) clarify the use of metaphors in psychotherapy as 'a symbolic attitude, which makes possible an experience of transition from lesser to greater awareness of the previously unconscious forces at work, which are disturbing current events and behaviour.'

In psychotherapeutic work with psychotic persons reality and fantasy are not regarded as being in opposition to one other. When one has to deal with delusive ideas, attempts are made to find their symbolic significance, and to follow them back in time. Fairy tales are full of magic and therefore they come close to the psychotic way of thinking, hearing and feeling, as seen, for example, in hallucinations.

A young female patient in the hospital wanted to get in contact with one of the staff members because, she said, 'she has got the key to the truth.' Apparently, the patient had responded to a copy of a piece of Viking jewelry – a silver key on a chain – which the woman was wearing. The concrete key had a particular significance for her, symbolizing access to the truth. What the truth implied to her, we do not know, only that she needed help from someone else. Since there are many doors, shrines and caves to open in fairy tales, leading to gold and diamonds symbolizing inner qualities in the hero rather than material values, it seemed likely that fairy tale therapy could be a way of approaching her.

In her book on fairy tales, J.C. Cooper (1984, p.130) writes about the soul reflected in the fairy tale: 'The more advanced belief is that the soul is the real *person* and the body its temporary manifestation. The primitive assumption is that the soul is attached to the body and that the body will live while the soul lives'. The soul can be kept separately for safe keeping and is best left guarded in some secure place, where it does not undergo the dangers and risks to which the body is exposed. Cooper also illustrates the idea of the separate soul – the belief that the soul can leave the body in sleep and maintain a separate existence in life, although it finally leaves the body at death.

In fairy tales we often find that the hero or heroine dies, being killed, eaten, cut to pieces and in a miraculous way wakes up to new life. It is only the body that dies; the spirit is still there. In trying to fly from the third floor of a house, a woman was seriously injured. Our immediate reaction on hearing this will probably be something like 'she must have been crazy'. If, however, we think of the heroine in the fairy tale who has to die to attain a new and better life, the woman still seems to have been in great danger, but she is no longer so far away from us. We seem to understand a little bit.

In work with symbols it is natural to pay attention to perception, imagination and memory, while including all our sensual impressions such as seeing, hearing, feeling, smelling etc. A visual impression, such as a key, could be a potential symbol when referring to a psychodynamic interpretation. This implies that we experience the key not only as a tool, but also with symbolic implications. In fairy tales, symbols appear as individuals, objects and events. As I see it, the potential symbol has informative value, which can be transformed by the unconscious into sets of drives. These are the instinct of self preservation, the libidinous drives, the intellectual drives and the spiritual drives.

The instinct of self preservation is related to any type of behaviour which tends to prolong the life of an organism, in particular by warding off an acute peril. It includes the drive to satisfy needs such as thirst and hunger. Seen in a broader perspective, it has to do with the wish to survive and thus the acceptance of development and change. This involves physiological change as well as psychological change growing out of increasing age and a changing way of life.

The libidinal drives have to do with libido, which is the dynamic expression or aspect of the sexual instinct related to the ego and to external objects or persons. It includes social wants and longings in their various aspects.

Intellectual drives should be looked upon in a very broad sense. They include the urge to do scientific research as well as the wishes to compose music, paint, write poetry and grow vegetables in a garden. Sometimes the expression 'achievement drives' is used. Curiosity is essential in relation to the intellectual drives and curiosity is apparent even in very small children. Spiritual drives have to do with the search or longing for a religion, a deeper understanding or insight, numinosity.

When people are prevented from satisfying their drives, the natural reaction will be anger and frustration. The expression of aggression can be seen in the small child and in the adult – although, of course, manifestation of aggression will vary depending on age, personality and life style. When there is no hope of having drives satisfied at any time, the consequence of striving without achieving goals can be alienation.

A potential symbol can have a positive stimulating effect leading to feelings of satisfaction; a negative stimulating effect leading to feelings of anger, fear, tension, and the wish to withdraw; and a conflicting stimulating effect leading to ambivalent feelings. The symbols activating our drives have a regulating impact on our actions like a stop and go mechanism, even if we are not aware of this. The influence of the unconscious on our drives is probably much stronger than we think it is.

Through the concept of archetypes, Jung has illustrated that some symbols apparently have an almost universal significance. It is also important to emphasize that a symbol can be interpreted in many ways, depending on the story in which the symbol appears, and on the individual experiencing the symbol.

Impressions do not always activate the unconscious, at least not as far as we can see. Perceptions can give us general information, as happens when the principle of logos is in focus. A key will normally be seen as a tool which can help to open a door, not often as a means of access to truth as was the case with the psychotic woman. Apparently, the key had a positive symbolic value for her, whereas it may have negative symbolic value for a person who has been locked up in prison or a closed ward in a psychiatric hospital.

However, the unconscious may also be excluded because of an inner conflict; one would then talk about a defence mechanism such as repression being activated, and we use the expression 'perceptual defence', which implies an unconscious protection from seeing, hearing and feeling.

We know that emotional involvement, including the stimulation of the unconscious, can sharpen our memory. If we go back to our childhood, some of our clearest memories will be attached to strong emotional experiences. If we have had too many frightening experiences as children, we are likely to develop perceptual defence mechanisms, which prevent us from seeing and hearing many things. Our emotions do not become activated either, and this protection can disturb our potential to learn, and later our memory, leading to intellectual alienation (Brun 1992). Thus one might say that stimulating the experience of potential symbols stimulates the unconscious. This again results in the activation of emotions, which increases the potential to learn, sets associations free and adds colour and strength to our experience of living.

Symbols in fairy tales are helpful. The individual symbol will be protected by the organization of the whole story, as described by Holbek (1987): 'The symbolic elements in fairy tales give emotional impressions of individuals, phenomena and happenings in the real world, given as a matter of fact description.' Fairy tales are not in any way sentimental, and the sensitive person is protected by the fact that feelings and emotions appear through the symbols; in this way they are not as immediate as if they were illustrated more directly. It is also a protection that the magic takes place within fairly strict frames. You know where you start and you have a feeling of where you are going to end, so if you meet three sons all wishing to marry the princess, you can be sure that it will be the youngest who will get her.

How is the Symbolic World Created?

According to experimental developmental psychology, it seems likely that babies have a differentiated ability to form symbols. Infants who are just a few weeks old show signs of intentions to speak. Soon after this, they engage in well organized, sometimes even humorous conversation with adults (Trevarthen 1975, p.227). Associated with this are distinctive 'handwaving' movements. These seem to be developmentally related to the gestures or gesticulations of adults in conversation. As early as the second month, a baby may imitate a mouth movement of the mother, thus showing that it has a model of the mother's face in the brain, and this model must be properly mapped into the motor apparatus of its own face.

Winnicott (1975) has developed the concept of transitional objects. These start as rituals carried out by babies, when satisfying basic needs. It could be a movement repeated by the child when sucking milk. This ritual becomes part of the experience and a symbol of it, a symbol which the child can recall when it becomes frustrated. On this basis early fantasies develop. At first, Winnicott thinks, they represent the mother's breast, later the child develops transitional phenomena and objects in play, art and culture. Winnicott also talks about potential space, which is synonymous with a capacity to tolerate illusion. Potential space develops out of a process of separation from the mother. As the mother gradually distances herself from the infant, the infant's growing capacity to manipulate symbols and thus create representations of the absent mother help the child in its further development. The playing aspect in this growth process is probably very important, if the growing child is to keep its creative strength as an adult (see Smith 1990).

Torsten Ingemann Nielsen (1986) has written about what he calls a symbolizing way of experiencing the world. He talks about something which is quite different, the numinous, the holy. He refers to a sensual, emotional and intuitive way of getting into contact with the symbolic way of experiencing and understanding art from different periods and cultures. We can experience the numinous in some of our dreams, if we allow ourselves to be sensitive to images and symbols.

Through studies of religions, myths, fairy tales, various forms of artistic ways of expressing feelings or ideas throughout the centuries, and through the studies of our dreams and fantasies, it is apparent that the symbolizing way of experiencing and recognizing is important to man, and we are surprised to find symbolic expressions very much like each other from very different cultures. Fairy tales have archetypal content. They are a world of symbols. Since symbols have a close connection with the unconscious, one might say that symbols related to the unconscious derive from archaic modes of psychic functioning.

In Contact with Important Symbols

In a way, fairy tales are concrete, so emotional qualities have to be expressed through attributes or actions. One might, however, say that the hero in the fairy tale is an abstraction, since he becomes in a way simplified and idealized – very different from that which characterizes a real person.

Feelings and reactions from the hero occur as things and events in the world around him – explained by Holbek (1987) as *projection* – so abstract ideas become illustrated through concrete objects with symbolic implications. These symbols have a strong impact on us because they stimulate imagination, which again call on our feelings and emotions. If the heroine feels that she is not treated well, this will often, according to Holbek, become illustrated in a way which shows us the mother as a stepmother or even a witch.

Magic presents could express the persons's characteristics. We see the heroine's good character through her combing gold and silver out of her hair, and she is wearing pearls, where the stepsister is spitting toads. This has been explained as *externalisation* (Holbek 1987).

Phallic aspects of the hero's character can be illustrated through swords, hammers, flutes. As for women, golden apples, rings, or shoes symbolize her feminine character, and often women and water become associated with each other (Holbek 1987).

When aspects of bodies, things or events turn up as independent symbolic elements, Holbek talks about *pars pro toto* – a part standing for the whole. Sometimes, conflicting aspects of the hero are split into different bodies (Dr Jekyll and Mr Hyde). In *Cinderella* we have the good and the wicked mother-image. The good mother is in the grave, the wicked mother is the stepmother, described by Holbek as *splitting*. Another frequent separation is seen in the split between the body and the soul. The hero sees the princess as an animal during the day and a human being during the night, or as animal first and later as a human being. A split is also seen in the separation between the very good old king and the frightful troll, the poor Cinderella and the queen of the ball, the beautiful queen and the witch trying to kill Snow White.

Since the fairy tale does not express itself through abstract means, still stronger or more intense feelings will be expressed in fairy tales through the *principle of quantification:* three heads, three dragons, etc. The time perspective in fairy tales will often be illustrated through abrupt changes. We don't know much about what happened during the 100 years during which Briar Rose was sleeping. This principle Holbek explains as *contraction* (Holbek 1987).

Cox and Theilgaard (1987) have written about the Aeolian Mode of dynamic psychotherapy in which an aesthetic imperative augments the patient's access to his inner world. 'The therapist catalyses this process by means of *poiesis* [which] is the process of calling something into existence that was not there before'. In their comprehensive book they are concerned with primary process material of special significance for the Aeolian Mode. They describe the presence of mutual contradiction, displacement, condensation, timelessness, *pars pro toto* thinking and the replacement of external by internal reality. Manifestations of primary process thinking occur in our dreams, fantasies and very often in psychotic thinking. Holbek (1989) shows that fairy tales are rich with primary process material, and thus form a link between external and internal reality. 'Primary process thinking deals with registration of sameness, identity and homogeneity, where secondary process thinking deals with discrimination of differences and heterogeneity' (Cox and Theilgaard 1987, p.195).

Reading psychoanalytically-oriented literature dealing with fairy tale inter-pretation, one meets interpretations of the various symbols, and the question arises, how can we be sure that the symbolic interpretation is correct? It is important to emphasize that the different symbols in the fairy tale interact and may have a reinforcing influence on one other. Besides, the individual symbol must be interpreted through an analysis of the whole story. The same symbol can thus have different interpretative values, depending on the context. In this way, fairy tale interpretation could be compared with dream interpretation. One has to be familiar with the context of the story to understand. An apple can be a positive feminine symbol illustrating fertility, but it also can be poisonous, a potential killer, as happens in *Snow White*. In fairy tale therapy, one also has to be sensitive to the significance of the symbols for the individual patient, who also makes his own relationships within the symbolic world; and lastly, it is important to be familiar with one's own symbolic world.

There are many ways to go when interpreting symbols. Holbek analyzed several versions of the fairy tale *The Princess on the Glass Mountain*. He was interested in finding out who had placed the princess on top of the glass mountain. He found that, in one version it was the troll, and in another version it was the father; he concluded that the troll and the father must be the same.

Having become familiar with the symbolic interpretation of fairy tales, and their archetypal qualities – through which one becomes aware that the process of reaching maturity in the young adult is illustrated through the hero's long journey and many trials, before he wins the princess and shows us that he has developed his *anima* – it is important to be sensitive to one's own interpretations, feelings and ideas. One must work with symbolic values in an individual way in order to give them life. To approach an understanding, it is helpful to try to be faithful to personal childhood memories, if possible before starting to try to explain anything to oneself. It is important to get in touch with spontaneous and naive feelings, to listen again and to see. The visual and concrete character, which is found in even the most magic fairy tale is what children like about them.

Reassuring feelings about fairy tales is a good basis, if one chooses to include them in the psychotherapeutic process, where it is necessary to be sensitive to the patient's interpretations. Working with fairy tales is very much working with symbols.

The Significance of Symbols in Everyday Life

I shall try to illustrate through two examples the significance of a symbol in different situations in daily life. In both cases, the symbol of a seal seemed to have a reassuring or healing function. 'The symbol carries an affective loading and symbolic expression integrates two modes, which reflect processes linked to the duality of the brain,' as explained by Cox and Theilgaard (1987, p.135). The symbols were positive in both cases, stimulating libidinal drives in the first story and, in the second story, also the instinct for self preservation.

A pregnant woman had a dream. She went down to the beach. She was standing there naked, enjoying the sunset, when suddenly a seal came up from the water and jumped into her arms. She could feel the soft skin touching her naked body, and the dream filled her with pleasure and calm. The dream was still clear in her mind many years later. Apparently she had not then known that in Nordic myths the seal is seen as a creature that can change into a human being for a short period. I quote from the myth from the Faero islands called *The Sealwoman*.

> 'He had not waited long when he noticed a whole lot of seals swimming towards the rocks. They managed to get on to the rocks one after another. Now Torkil saw something, he had never seen before. Every seal slipped out of its skin and became a human being. There were men as well as women, he heard their laughter. He also could hear them talking to each other, as he approached the rock' (Nielsen 1983, p.10).

In the story, the man falls in love with a sealwoman. He takes her skin away, which prevents her from changing into a seal again. She is very unhappy, but has to marry him, and they have children. One day he forgets his key, and the sealwoman finds her skin, which has been locked up. She disappears into the water, and he cannot find her. Walking down to the beach he sees a seal looking at him and his children with longing eyes.

The seal in the pregnant woman's dream could very well symbolize the child she was expecting. It came from the sea, the symbol of the unconscious and of the great Mother. The symbol of the seal could also illustrate the development and change which takes place during pregnancy and childbirth. The experience of the sensual feeling of the soft skin, when she held the seal in her arms, clearly met with her libidinous wishes and drives.

The woman who dreamed this had her baby, and when her daughter was eighteen years old, it was time for the young woman to leave home. When the child grows up, the mother has to withdraw her projections gradually, as explained by von Franz (1987).

In the myth the man tried to prevent the sealwoman from leaving him, when she was changing into a seal, but he could not, and mothers have to accept that their children change and become adults. The mother knew that her daughter should live her own independent life, but emotionally she was not quite there. However, when confronted with the story about 'the seal woman' she remembered her dream of the seal of many years ago. She had a vague feeling that already then she had felt the limited time perspective; she could only be with 'the seal' (the baby) for a fairly short period of life. The image of the seal helped her to realize emotionally that she should be careful not to hold on to her daughter. It became easier for her to let her go.

The symbolic significance of the seal seemed clear also in the following story. Some years ago, I was going to a meeting in Jutland. Most of the way I went by train, and then I got a taxi for the last part. The driver was a woman in her forties. We were talking about the weather, and the place I was going to, when suddenly she said: 'Really I should not have been alive.' I got a strange feeling. You are very much dependent on the driver, when you are in a taxi, and what did she mean by this apparently very important message? She explained that she had been born much too early, and her identical twin sister had died when she was only a few days old. She herself had to stay in hospital for a long time as a baby, and the doctors and nurses had not given her parents much hope that she would survive, but she did. She was still very small and weak when she left hospital. As she grew up, she always had a strange longing for the sister she never saw, her dead twin sister. As an adult, she sometimes got the feeling that she had to go to her sister's grave, even though she had never known her. Her family did not understand her reactions in this situation. Recently, she had celebrated her birthday, and on that day her now grown up daughter had given her a toy seal, very white and soft. She had not asked for one, but by a strange coincidence she also got a toy seal from her older brother. Apparently, her two relatives had not talked to each other about their unusual birthday presents which recreated a pair of identical twins.

I told her that her longing for the dead twin sister was a natural feeling, even though she had not known her twin sister. Identical twins parted from one another, even as very small children, will frequently try to find their lost sister or brother, since their longing is very strong. As I saw the gifts from her daughter and brother, they illustrated that somehow her family members were beginning to understand her. This was also what she had felt, although they had not talked about her twin sister when she celebrated her birthday.

Quite some time after this, I came across *The Sealwoman*, and I thought of the female taxi-driver, whose choice of job seemed on a symbolic level to illustrate her continual travelling to find her lost sister. The myth in the Faero Islands may very well have had something to do with people losing family members – husbands, sons, daughters. They may have disappeared due to a shipwreck or have taken their own lives. When people in sorrow have walked down to the sea, which took human lives, they have seen the seals with their very human, somehow longing eyes.

The seal has become an archetypal symbol influencing the unconscious drives, as is true with the brother and the daughter of the taxi driver, when they selected a toy seal to meet with the woman's libidinous drives and her instinct of self preservation according to a psychodynamic interpretation. When she lost her baby sister, she lost something of herself, since the identity of identical twins is very closely attached to the other. There is magic power in symbols and fairy tales, and even if we have to be very careful not to turn psychotherapy into magic formulas and suggestion, we should include the potential healing power in significant symbols when they are taken in at the right moment.

Symbols within the Psychotherapeutic Sphere

From these two examples of symbols in everyday life, we will go to the psychotherapeutic situation, where symbols with a special significance frequently turn up in the minds of psychotic people. If we as professionals are aware of this, we may share a symbolic attitude, sometimes allowing ourselves to introduce symbols which we feel could be helpful just on a particular day at a particular moment. Milton Erickson has used the expression 'mental suggestion', which may lead to an unconscious change (see Lundgren and Norrby 1988).

Kirsty, a disturbed young female patient, had lived in a destructive feminine universe since she was a child. One day she brought a drawing with her when seeing me with a male nurse. It was a pentameter – a pentagonal star – and she had drawn seven children inside. She had made the children first and then the star. We talked about the protective function of a star. The nurse had told both of us how in the olden days people used to have a star over the door to protect them against nightmares. He told us that one evening when he was on duty, a female patient could not fall asleep. She came to his office, obviously feeling uneasy, so he said:'Perhaps you need a pentameter to protect you,' and he illustrated his idea by drawing a star on a piece of paper. The woman took the paper and went to bed. Later he found her sleeping with the drawing placed on her breast.

Kirsty asked: 'Did you give her the drawing?' And he answered 'No I just made it, put it on the table, and then she took it with her'. Kirsty smiled. It was as if she felt it reassuring that the woman did not have to take the star. It was not given to her, but she chose to pick it up herself. One migh also say that the woman had not been persuaded to do something, rather she had decided for herself. It seems so important when introducing symbols in psychotherapy that we are careful in our ways of presenting them. They should not be given as a gift, or forced into the patient's mind; better to show where they are in case they might be of help, just as happened with the woman who fell asleep with a pentameter. She had picked it up on her own initiative. One also has to be careful, when working with the symbols introduced by the patient, never to go further with the symbol than the patient is ready to go. This means listening carefully to one's own intuition.

One day Kirsty brought a drawing to the psychotherapeutic session. It was a bird flying; its head was drooping. She had drawn the bird very lightly, but inside you could see a red heart. In the upper corner of the paper was a small drawing of a bird fixed to the paper. It appeared that she had been talking to one of the nurses about her drawing at a time when she had not got it with her. To make him understand she had made a small illustrative sketch, and he suggested to her that she should bring it with her for the next session, having fixed the small drawing to the big one, so both drawings would be there.

The bird had a heart attack, she said. It was flying over the woods and the sea, and she did not know where it would fall down when it died. On the small drawing you could see that the head of the bird was not drooping quite so much as on the big one. We had worried about the patient for some time, since she seemed depressed, and we feared she might regress into psychosis.

The heart contains the soul, which one might see as a fire in the hearth of the heart. Sick of heart is sickness of the soul and of the body's vital energy. This is what might come to mind when confronted with the drawing made by the female patient. A bird having a heart attack and being in danger of falling into the woods or into the sea could be interpreted as a risk of regression into psychosis.

The bird looked like a swallow, and so it felt natural for the psychotherapist to think of Thumbelina in the fairy tale by Hans Christian Andersen. Thinking of Thumbelina, we talked about the small girl carefully looking after the swallow for the whole winter, although it looked dead. When the winter was over and spring was coming the swallow woke up and, lifting its head, it did not forget that Thumbelina had taken such good care of it. Going back to the drawings it seemed hopeful that the bird on the small drawing had lifted its head just a tiny bit. Many months later we returned to the drawings and the patient said: 'You have also taken care of me' referring to the members of the staff. Gradually, she became able to work with feelings and reactions in her life which were very difficult to talk about, by referring to fairy tales in her drawings.

Applying the Rorschach ink blot test as a projective technique, which can be valuable in a diagnostic process which is trying to find out what kind of therapy might be helpful for an individual patient, one is often confronted with the significance of symbols presented by the patient (McCully 1971). If you, as a therapist, remember these strong pictures and try to understand some of their dynamic significance; they may be helpful later in a psychotherapeutic process.

A very young female patient gave the following interpretation as her first to Plate I in the Rorschach test: 'There are angel wings with a monster inside'. This image seemed to illustrate her emotional disturbance and confusion very clearly. Angel wings normally have associations with a positive, harmonious, reassuring and protecting experience in our culture; but what if you find that there is a monster behind? To integrate different aspects of our character, to face sometimes conflicting personality traits in ourselves, we must be able to make a differentiation or separation; so, as I saw it, it might be important with this young woman to work with symbols such as the good fairy and the troll, just as they are found in fairy tales.

Working with the fairy and with the troll would mean that one did not exclude the very disturbed and destructive drives in her, but one would try to make her see the world as less confusing. The small vicious troll living in the dark forest might represent aspects of the child's character which the child sees as vicious and selfish in herself. As expressed by Birkhäuser-Oeri (1988, p.23), 'to deal with the shadow one must be able to assess good and evil and differentiate between them'. The process of individuation has to do with a gradual confrontation with one's shadow side, which gives the possibility of setting free unrealised potentials. This young woman had been characterized as 'an as-if personality'. She could adapt through imitation to situations and other people, but she would suddenly react in a very disturbed and destructive way. She was either very good or very bad, like the fairy in *Peter Pan* who was so small that she could only contain one feeling at a time. This young woman did not, apparently, understand her disturbed reactions; her insight was poor, and having reacted in a destructive way, she had no apparent guilt feelings afterwards. She did not feel responsible for her own deeds. One might also say that she was in a state of mind which she could not reflect upon, having left it, so that her perspective of time was also disturbed, and so was her instinct for self preservation. Since it was so difficult for her to get in touch with her real feelings, it seemed important to create contact with symbols calling on emotions that do not come too close.

Conclusion

In fairy tales the hero often makes many mistakes before he reaches his goal. According to psychoanalytic literature, this illustrates a maturational process. People who plan their lives very carefully, trying always to do the most sensible things, may lose some of their inner life and imagination. It is part of our development to make mistakes, and it is sometimes quite healthy to do so. This is what fairy tales tell us. In crises in our lives, where we tend to focus on what went wrong, the many foolish actions in fairy tales can help us reach a balance, and achieve a more tolerant and sometimes also a clearer attitude towards ourselves.

It is encouraging that the youngest and the least esteemed son wins the princess. It gives us hope, and it can be reassuring to think that some silly things that we have done in our lives may have been the only thing we could have done at that particular moment.

CHAPTER 2

The Use of Fairy Tales in Psychotherapy

Birgitte Brun

Introduction

An increasing number of books concerning psychodynamic fairy tale interpretation and psychotherapy through fairy tales are coming out these days. It is as if fairy tales are in the air.

There may be many explanations for this. Marie Louise von Franz (1987), the Jungian author and psychoanalyst, who has been an expert on fairy tale interpretation for many years, has pointed out that we are constantly and habitually trained from the very beginning to repress our personal emotional reactions and to train our mind to be what we call objective. In this so called objective world, where science and technology play a very important part in our lives, we need something different, which may stimulate emotional experiences, early childhood memories and imagination. Fairy tales bring us into contact with preconscious longings and aspirations; they extend reality beyond the daily sometimes quite narrow world.

Judith Hubback (1990, p.79) has expressed it in this way: 'There is a distinction between, on the one hand, the experiental way of apprehending the world and its contents, and on the other hand the contrasted ways: the immediate, the intuitive and (for some) the religious.'

T.I. Nielsen (1986) calls our attention to Julian Jaynes' neuropsychological hypothesis related to the fact that the two hemispheres have different functions, and that normally the left hemisphere is dominant. Jaynes' theory is that once man was able to hear the voices of the gods. These voices came from the right hemisphere and they moved to the left hemisphere, the hemisphere of language. Gradually, man developed abilities in introspection and autonomous thinking and acting, so the gods lost their influence. Their voices disappeared, and the left hemisphere became dominant while the right one was quieter.

Sociologists have found a new way of referring to the youngest generation, they call it the yes-no generation, characterized by a digital way rather than an analogue way of thinking. The digital computerworld-inspired way of thinking has to do with either or, very sharp and precise statements. The analogue way seems more complicated, emotional and multi-faceted (Blum 1991). The analogue way of thinking is what we find in fairy tales.

The American folklorist S. Thompson defines a fairy tale as 'A tale of some length involving a succession of motifs or episodes. It moves in an unreal world without definite locality and definite characters, and is filled with the marvellous. In this never never land humble heroes kill adversaries, succeed to kingdoms and marry princesses. The fairy tale is a poetical vision of the human being and its relation to the world. For centuries this vision has given strength and confidence to the listeners, because they have felt the inner truth from it.'

All European people know and love the formula 'Der var engang – Es war einmal – il y avait une fois – once upon a time'. In Hungary, the story teller brings you to a place which no one can control, so that it may start like this: 'Once upon a time, I do not know where, behind seven times seven kingdoms and still longer away also behind the enormous sea next to a collapsed oven, was an old woman, etc' (see Christensen 1976).

The hero's journey often goes through suffering and loss; only those who have experienced great danger and known the reality of death become complete persons. Suffering and disaster are not solely harmful, but lead to maturity. When we come to the end of the fairy tale, we hear that 'they lived happily ever after' and in addition we may add 'and if they have not died, they are still alive.'

The brothers Grimm looked upon fairy tales as something surviving from the common Germanic world of myths. Others have claimed that almost all our fairy tales come from India, and from there they have gradually wandered to Europe. The Celts have given us some very old and good fairy tales. We have fairy tales from Egypt going back to two thousand B.C. Italy was the first country in Europe to have collections of fairy tales (Brostrøm 1987). There are theories expressing the opinion that almost identical fairy tales may have turned up in several places almost simultaneously. One well known collection of fairy tales is that of Charles Perraut. The first collection came out in 1694 and consisted of two fairy tales in verse.

Folk tales are classified in different ways. Thompson (1955–58) identifies five groups

1. Animal tales.

2. Ordinary folk tales, including tales of magic, religious tales, romantic tales, tales of the stupid ogre.

3. Jokes and anecdotes.

4. Formula tales with rhymes and repetitions.

5. Unclassified tales.

Even where the stories are found in a written form, they still have strong oral qualities. They are therefore good to read aloud or retell (Brostrøm 1987). In this way they become naturally linked with psychotherapy, in which the spoken language plays such an important role. In *Myths and Fairy Tales*, Heuscher (1974) has pointed out what Jung stressed in looking at a dream, or a hallucinatory experience. In a myth or a fairy tale, the various characters appearing in them show different aspects or qualities of the protagonist. So when the prince (and the right prince) gets the princess, we are not only confronted with the union of man and woman, but we also follow a process whereby the man meeting the princess has developed his anima and thus reached a mature mental stage. In other words, the princess should be looked upon as illustrating symbolic aspects of the prince's character. If we follow the heroine, a princess, her marriage to the prince will express a realization of her animus.

Amongst fairy tale interpreters and psychoanalysts who have applied fairy tales in their psychotherapeutic and psychoanalytic work there are two traditional schools. These are the Jungian school and the Freudian school. I mention them in this order, because the tradition is strongest within the Jungian school with authors such as Julian Heuscher (1974), M.L. von Franz (1987) Sibylle Birkhäuser-Oeri (1988), Katrin Asper (1989) Verena Kast (1989) and the Danish Jungian psychoanalyst Eigil Nyborg. Nyborg's book on Hans Christian Andersen's fairy tales came out in Danish as early as 1962.

Probably the best known book is Bruno Bettelheim's *The Uses of Enchantment*, published in 1976, following the Freudian tradition. Bettelheim emphasizes that the fairy tale is imaginative and a story on two levels. On one level it is entertaining, and on the second level it speaks directly to the unconscious mind. It contains four elements, fantasy, recovery from deep despair, escape from some great danger, but most of all consolation. All four elements are important in psychotherapy.

Many authors have tried to make systematic interpretations of symbols as is described by Holbek in his comprehensive work *Interpretation of Fairy Tales* (1987). Holbek does not think such interpretations possible, since the significance of the individual symbol depends on the context. On symbols, he writes: 'They seem to be ambivalent, or better, polyvalent, since their meanings are related rather than mutually opposed'. These words seem very important within a psychotherapeutic perspective. In relation to psychotherapy, one might say that only if the symbols get life will they be helpful in the psychotherapeutic process. The patient and the psychotherapist should become able to relate to the symbol and from this a mutual understanding develops. The therapist will always have to look upon the symbol in its context, applying a gestalt-psychological approach. None the less, we have given illustrations of a few symbols in the end of this book in the hope of providing some inspiration.

Verena Kast (1989) writes in her book about fairy tales in psychotherapy: 'If you succeed at the right moment to find the right fairy tale, the psychotherapeutic process will become intensified or a stand still in the psychotherapeutic process may be overcome' (1989, p.11). She also points out that the therapeutic process changes if the analyst or psychotherapist introduces a fairy tale into the psychotherapeutic process with a patient. The two people will then both be involved with the fairy tale, the focus of attention will change, no longer being concentrated on the patient quite so directly. The fairy tale or symbols in the story will be between the two – and to some patients this is quite a relief. It is as if they can feel their problems in a larger context.

Fairy tales have individual significance and they are universal. The universal or archetypal significance can provide a protection when it is difficult to face personal conflicts. Many people, whether they are neurotic, borderline, or persons living through a crisis, express anxiety when talking about their feelings, dreams and wishes. Even within the protected situation which characterizes psychotherapy, they find it very hard to talk about their thoughts, despair and longings. They are afraid to reveal what they sometimes describe as the chaos inside. Feelings of envy, hate and jealousy can be heavily burdened with shame and guilt feelings and therefore be difficult to express. Quite often in our professional lives we meet people who have never really had the chance to reflect upon their own lives with an attentive person sitting by, so psychotherapy may seem strange or even mysterious to them.

Sometimes a patient will express the fear that the psychotherapist might feel contempt and push him away if what he had been doing was known. Sometimes it is not even a matter of doing, but merely of thinking or feeling. He is afraid to reveal dark aspects of his character. If one tries to confront him directly with this conflict, or approach themes which one thinks are important, he may become frightened, with the result that he becomes even more worried and withdrawn.

It can be helpful in such a situation for the therapist to become more active, which gives the patient the feeling that the therapist is not as observant as he might have thought. In other words, one tries to make him feel more at ease. There are, of course, many ways of doing this, depending on the patient's personality and on what comes naturally to the individual psychotherapist. One approach would be to move towards what one thinks is the difficult area of conflict by talking about another person, who had a similar problem. But one might also choose to tell a story or encourage him to read a story or fairy tale which will afterwards be shared with him. In this situation it is, of course, natural to choose a fairy tale which somehow illustrates his problems. This may not necessarily be a fairy tale he likes, or a fairy tale with healing power. It could be one that is helpful in identifying his problems, stimulating fantasies and memories – images, one might say – showing a path to approaching what seems frightening and burdened with feelings which are hard to face.

One might say that the fairy tale becomes an indirect way to approach themes that are difficult to talk about. The concept of using a story to get in touch with a problem can be illustrated by taking an example from everyday life with a small child. In this case the story was not a fairy tale, but one that was parallel to the little girl's daily life.

> Heidi, a girl of two years old, had got into the habit of scratching other children in her nursery-school. This caused a good deal of trouble, and the staff spoke to her parents about it and asked them to do something to make her stop. Of course, the little girl might be having a difficult time for various reasons, and it seemed important for her parents to try to find out what could be wrong. As well as trying to discover objectively what made their daughter feel uncomfortable or insecure, increasing her inner tension, they tried to talk to her about it. Although she was very articulate for her age, she reacted by walking away if they started to touch on the subject. She would just not show any interest, which is quite natural, since it was a conflicting theme. One day, her father told her a story about a small Swedish girl he knew, whose name was Hilde. She lived in a family which, interestingly enough, was very similar to Heidi's family. He talked quite a lot about Hilde, who had many friends, but sometimes nobody wanted to play with her, because she scratched them. Heidi listened attentively, and she showed interest in hearing about Hilde and about her scratching the other children. In this way her own situation could be approached gently and gradually. For Heidi it seemed easy to identify with Hilde who was so much like her.

In the psychotherapeutic world, we meet people who don't allow themselves to have lively fantasies. They find it difficult to express themselves through drawing, painting, music, dance, drama or whatever it might be; nor do they take part in cultural rituals, which could set free some of their energy and release feelings. If they are encouraged to talk about their dreams, they will very likely answer that they don't dream or they cannot remember any dreams.

Bruce L. Smith (1990), has developed the idea of potential space initially articulated by D. Winnicott. Potential space refers to a metaphoric zone of psychological experience, an intermediate area between reality and fantasy, the location of symbolic thought, play and cultural experience. The potential space is synonymous with a capacity to tolerate illusion and develops out of the process of separation from the mother. Where the child's separation from the mother has been traumatic, the child will experience the space between self and other as frightening, void, an emptiness that cannot be filled or symbolized. This can be the case with persons suffering from psychosomatic illnesses. It also can be the case with 'nomopathic' patients who suffer from an impoverishment of expression and lack of curiosity, liveliness and spontaneity. It is as if fantasy is missing from the psyche altogether.

In this situation, it can be helpful to provide a person with pictures and to stimulate memories – not necessarily very personal memories, since these often provoke defensive reactions, but memories that they share with many other people.

To recall or search one's memory for a fairy tale which one may not have thought of for many years is a subjective and personal experience which is, however, protected by the story itself. Sometimes it is also comforting to think that one can always return to the story, if associations take one too far away from the start and cause too much anxiety. Fairy tales are important because they provide an easy and natural access to the visual world, which may also form a bridge between past and present. They sometimes revive acoustic memories based on rhythms and rhymes in such fairy tales as *Peter Rabbit* 'going lippity, lippity not very fast, and looking all around.' The stories may evoke bodily sensations; that is, a person may remember the sensations in his body which were there when he first heard the story. Sometimes, the memories become so strong that it is like experiencing the fairy tale again.

With personal and private memories, people in psychotherapy will sometimes say that it is as if there is more to the story. They just cannot remember it. This, of course, may be due to repression; at a later stage they will sometimes dream and imagine more freely and will then remember. With the use of fairy tales, there is always the possibility of refreshing that part of the memory which is the actual story. The patient can read the fairy tale again, one can tell the story to him, give it to him to read or even read it aloud if that feels natural. In this way important memories can somehow be traced without intruding on more private spheres. The patient decides where to draw the line between the actual story and the way of experiencing it. The experience is his alone.

Fairy tales are part of our history, a cultural heritage which can help people create continuity in their lives and which give a feeling of mutuality. There is the possibility of there being a common basis of experience if both therapist and patient know the fairy tale, and there is the possibility of finding the patient in his childhood making contact with the therapist's childhood as well. This, of course, does not imply that the therapist starts to talk about personal childhood memories, but he gets personal access to the story, going back in time.

To help a person get into contact with the unconscious through dreams and fantasies seems important in psychotherapy. Fairy tales and their symbols can be helpful in this situation. If symbols in fairy tales have life during the psychotherapeutic process, they exist in the room, even if they are not talked about. Sometimes they call on emotions in a quicker and easier way than many words; they also live outside the psychotherapeutic room, since they are easy to move. The symbol has visual qualities, and it is a centre of energy connected with other symbols. Sometimes it is placed as a key concept in a whole story, where one knows the beginning – 'once upon a time' – and the end. It is somehow a comforting feeling to know that, even if one follows the hero through many dangers, there is a positive ending.

Verena Kast (1989) has pointed out that often in fairy tales solutions are found which one would not have thought possible. We say: 'It is like a fairy tale'. The fairy tale eases the future, which is important for us, if we are not to remain in the past.

Fairy tales are also special stories, since they come from a long story tradition. They start with a problem and show which processes have to be lived through before one can solve the problem. Often this has to do with general human problems. Bengt Holbek (1987) provides clear illustrations of the structure in magic fairy tales through the following five acts:

> Act I: Someone tells the hero not to do certain things. He breaks the law and gets punished, is taken away under the influence of magic, etc.

> Act II: The hero is given a task. He completes the task (and is rewarded) through the intervention of magic advice, abilities or helpers.

> *(Sometimes acts I and II are interchangeable: act I may be presented as a flash-back in act III)*

> Act III: the hero finds his future partner, and uses what he has achieved in act II.

> Act IV: Hero and/or heroine are persecuted, put into prison, they are given new challenges, they reach the future home or castle.

> Act V: There is help from the future partner. Things become revealed, the enemies punished. There is a wedding.

Feelings we do not like and have difficulty talking about may find a symbolic expression in a fairy tale. We get the necessary working distance, so to speak, because it is our picture and yet not our private picture, since we share it with other people.

Fairy tales can help us look upon our lives in a wider perspective. Fairy tales from very different parts of the world have the same symbolic qualities. This is helpful working with people whose mother tongue is different from the therapist's own, and if they have a cultural background which the therapist does not know very well. As Dundes (1982) shows, we find Cinderella stories in Europe, China, Eurasia, Africa, Tuscany, America and Russia. This means that, even if a patient comes from a part of the world which is alien, one has the ability to share experiences through a fairy tale such as *Cinderella*.

As we shall describe later, we sometimes sense a barrier, working in psychotherapy, with a language which the patient has mastered to a high degree, but did not know as a child. It is as if the 'foreign', though perfectly spoken, language is a protection from getting in touch with the wounded child. The new language is like a shield carried for safety. If one knows the original language, one may try to speak it. Often, however, the patient will not find this natural, and so it is no real help. In this situation, fairy tales told in his native tongue can get him back on the stage, if an old story is retold. The old story makes him listen to the words and music of the language, which was there from the very beginning of his life 'il y avait une fois'.

Dealing with psychotic people, one gets in touch with very disturbed feelings, ideas and behaviour. Then it can be helpful to be able to find similar ideas in fairy tales. In my experience it is helpful not only for the patient, but also for the therapist. As expressed in a letter from Bengt Holbek (1991) 'The difference between the creation of symbols in the mentally ill and symbols in fairy tales (and of course literature) could be explained through the fairy tale offering order, solutions of conflicts, a harmonious ending, whereas the sick fantasy has no such solution'.

Bettelheim (1976) expressed the idea that fairy tales are helpful to the child in its development: 'If a child is told only stories "true to reality" (which means false to important parts of his inner reality), then he may conclude that much of his inner reality is unacceptable to his parents. Many a child thus estranges himself from his inner life, and this depletes him. Therefore it may later, as an adolescent no longer under the emotional sway of its parents, come to hate the rational world and escape entirely into a fantasy world, as if to make up for what it lost in childhood. At an older age this could imply a severe break with reality, with all the dangerous consequences for the individual and society' (1976, p.65).

I found these words very true when I was working with a young delinquent man who had committed a serious crime. Neither his mother nor father (nor anyone else) ever read stories to him. He grew up with very few good childhood memories. As a teenager, he joined groups of delinquents who committed robberies. At a certain stage he developed omnipotent fantasies, where he saw it as part of his fate that he should commit a serious crime. No good experiences and feelings could balance his destructive fantasies, and when a friend suggested that he was just boasting, his fantasies were transformed into serious action.

He was not a fellow with whom one could sit and read a fairy tale, but it was through a positive symbol of the self in his otherwise very dramatic and anxiety-provoking dreams that we found a fragile basis on which to start. The picture was of a ball with which he was playing in his dream. Even while most of his dreams were terrifying nightmares, we could find the ball.

Bettelheim also emphasizes that if a person becomes alienated from the unconscious processes, he cannot use them to enrich his life in reality. As will be illustrated, fairy tales can be used to create an emotional contact. When focusing on fairy tales that have special significance for the individual in psychotherapy, his or her problems can be dealt with in a way that is sometimes less provoking and therefore less disturbing than if one uses more direct and confrontational methods. Therapist and patient have the opportunity to stay within a fairy tale world for a long time. From there one can step into the more personal and precarious existence and go back again to the fairy tale, which is sometimes safer ground.

Fairy Tales are for All of Us

This book deals with therapy and guidance through fairy-tales, and we have tried to discuss experiences that we have found important. As you will see, we have applied different methods in our work and the frames or settings in which we have worked have also varied.

One approach has to do with helping children to live with traumas and serious losses in their lives. Fairy tales may call upon good memories from time past. They stimulate fantasies, they give the child the chance to talk about difficulties in life without being too personal, and they create hope. This help can be given in the child's daily life by a sensitive adult person, not as actual psychotherapy, but as an emotional support. This gives the child the chance to gain a better understanding of his own lifestyle.

The Swiss psychoanalyst Kathrin Asper (1989) emphasizes that fairy tales deal with good and evil and thus very basic conditions in human life. She writes: 'The child not feeling that its parents love it becomes split into a "good" and a "bad" part. The good part represents itself as persona and identification, while the "bad" part includes the negative self-image with feelings like "I am bad (because I am not loved), I am guilty, feel sorry, insecure, empty inside, fright-ened"' (1989, p.130–131). Eigil Nyborg (1962) explains it as follows: 'The ideas about good and evil are probably as old as humans. The antagonists Christ and Satan are therefore archetypal images. We become confronted with two different images of the self, which are likely to represent a dualism. It is, however, as if originally there has been a substantial identity between these spiritual contrasts' (1962, p.130–131).

The good and the evil concern contrasts, which are part of life itself, since all that is alive is energy and dependent upon opposites. Good and evil determine each other, as is very clearly illustrated in fairy tales, which also help us to understand more about ourselves and other people.

Fairy tales with their archetypal images have fascinated people for centuries. There are still authors such as Campbell who, in *The Power of Myths* (1988) claim that fairy tales are for children. The most common attitude (expressed by Holbek (1987)) is that they have been created by adults and have started to circulate among adults. We may guess that children have often been interested partici-pants; that is another story. It is our experience that fairy tales can be used by everyone, whether they show interest from the start or whether they become interested later on.

Support for emotionally disturbed children including the use of fairy tales has been illustrated by the Norwegian psychologist P. J. Brudal (1984) of Gaustad's psychiatric hospital. His description of the use of fairy tales with emotionally disturbed children is not actual psychotherapy, but it has been an inspiration to psychotherapists working with fairy tales.

Through case-stories, he has tried to show us his method. One case concerns a nine-year-old boy who had to be held tight, sometimes for several hours, to prevent him destroying himself and everything around him. One day, having raged for about five hours, he suddenly got hold of a fairy tale book. He found a particular story and asked the social worker to read it to him. It was a story he already knew about 'mumble goose egg' a Norwegian story about a group of women who find a very big egg. They lie on it and out comes a huge boy. Before the boy has come out of the egg, they can hear him mumble about porridge and milk. That is why they call him mumble goose egg. This boy eats everything that the women have, so they send him away. Wherever he goes, he takes all the food and people get to be afraid of him. In the end he throws the king into heaven and marries his daughter.

The staff discussed why the boy seemed to calm down when he heard this fairy tale. They discovered that there were many parallels between the story and the boy's life. He had been an unwanted child, and his family did not like him. He was very greedy. This had to do with the fact that he had had too little to eat for long periods of his life. The third point was his obsessive preoccupation with strength, greatness and power.

The staff members discussed whether it could be of any help to a child to have his problems repeated by hearing a particular fairy tale. They decided to work with more children in a systematic way to find out what could be helpful, but before this they had a long talk. Would it be better if the adults helped the child to separate fantasies from reality? Would it be better to help the child control its own destructive emotions in the real concrete world?

The staff concluded that most of the day they tried to help children stick to reality. On this basis it seemed all right to leave a short time for fairy tale reading, during which the therapist approaches the child at a symbolic level, where the forbidden and difficult psychic conflicts and emotions come in and the child is confronted with these in a way which is not as provoking as if it were real life they were talking about.

The staff decided that, when they had become familiar with the children, they should read fairy tales in small groups during the evenings. Because of the many negative experiences which deprived children have had, it is sometimes difficult to create a positive relationship between the child and the adults in an institution. The child will project negative experiences onto the adults, which creates anxiety and uncertainty. Therefore, it may be easier for the child to identify with positive figures in the fairy tales, because the identification takes place on an imaginary level. According to Brudal, the introduction of a fairy tale can become a turning point in the development of a disturbed child.

In *The Healing Power of Fairy Tales*, the Swedish authors Lundgren and Borgström Norrby (1988) describe a special way of reading fairy tales to children, working with children with a physical illness in hospital for very long periods. They chose fairy tales which they thought would be helpful to the child and might have healing powers. They helped the children get in touch with their emotions and work through experiences in their lives which had been difficult for them. In the end, they created a fairy tale for each child, which somehow illustrated the child's life situation and gave them hope for the future. They told the story in the same way as they had told the other stories. They showed respect and did not try to make a very close emotional relationship with the child, which could be disturbing for the child when they had to leave each other, probably never to meet again. They encouraged the children to illustrate the fairy tales – a combination of supportive fairy tale therapy and art therapy.

As we have seen, fairy tales are universal and thus they may be of help to everyone – both children and adults. We have used fairy tales in the treatment of people in crisis, and patients with different kinds of personality disturbances, including schizophrenic patients. The actual diagnosis does not seem to have a great influence on the choice of using fairy tales in the work with a particular patient. It is more what happens in the sessions or does not happen, which makes us 'open the old picture-book', as we show later.

Ernst W. Pedersen's fairy-tale conversations are joint meetings with patients and staff-members. Quite a few patients and staff-members have been through these experiences, and the interest in fairy tales is increasing. Somehow, his work also prepares peoples' minds for later psychotherapy.

I visited a ward one day with very sick patients to inquire about a young schizophrenic man. He had been in bed for most of the day during the past weeks. He seemed to withdraw from contact, and could not speak to anyone. When I asked if there was nothing which might interest him, a nurse said that the day before there had been a fairy tale session. She had said that he could attend it if he liked, so he got out of bed and sat there for almost the whole session, apparently listening. What he was hearing we do not know, but he was there.

In Sct. Hans Hospital library, many people ask for fairy tale books. Some patients will make excuses saying 'I know they are for children, but they are easier for me to read than real books'. They get the answer 'Fairy tales are for all of us'.

Selection of Fairy Tales in Psychotherapy

One day, a young colleague of ours asked: 'How do you use fairy tales in psychotherapy? How can they be introduced? And which fairy tales would you choose?'

Before one can answer these questions, it is important to know what the therapist's own relationship with fairy tales is. Are fairy tales in any way important to her? If so, has she got a favourite story, and has she thought of the reasons why she likes this story best? Does she remember any fairy tales she did not like as a child, and has she any idea why this was so?

In other words, the first thing to do will be to tune into the subject and feel where one is in the landscape. Do you feel tempted to follow Hans of Luck, or would you prefer to walk with Little Red Ridinghood into the woods, where you will meet the wolf?

Why do you remember some fairy tales very clearly, whereas others have almost faded away, even if you know you have heard them quite often as a child? Do you know any old fairy tales that you would like to read again? What is your attitude, when reading fairy tales to children? How do you respond to their questions? It seems important to confront yourself with the past and present magic world, to start with.

According to the literature concerning fairy tale therapy, very many stories have been used over the years. So, in this respect, there is potentially a great variety. One way to start would be to ask the patient which fairy tale he likes most, and to use this information to include a particular story in the therapeutic process. However, as Cox and Theilgaard (1987) emphasize, when a subject is brought up, one should try to be very sensitive to the patient. If one asks such a question, it should be at the right time, where it really means something to him. The therapist should have the intuitive feeling that he is ready for it.

People who like to work with fairy tales are likely to listen with the magic ear. This means one is ready to catch the symbolic meaning of words. Sometimes one may think of a patient, perhaps even dream about him and his problems. Having almost given up hope of solving a particular problem, at least for the time being, one tends to relax. This provides space for unconscious energies; creative processes start and suddenly a key may be found through a fairy tale, or merely a figure or symbol in the story which comes to mind.

When a psychotherapist becomes interested in using fairy tales, patients will often feel it, even if it is not talked about. They may refer to fairy tale symbols in a way that starts the process. Sometimes they will talk about dreams that could naturally be associated with fairy tales. If a person feels lonely with an anxiety-provoking dream, the association with the fairy tale can make him feel less lonely. It can help him see the dream as illustrating conflicts that are common to many people.

Verena Kast uses group psychotherapy in which she integrates fairy tales. She chooses a story and reads it to the group, choosing a story that she finds essential to that particular group. In her book she describes the stages in psychotherapy, starting with reading a fairy tale. Later, she works with the associations this has for different members of the group. They can work for several sessions with the themes from a single story, moving through different processes. In fairy tale psychotherapy there are two basic attitudes. One has to do with identifying problems and conflicts, the other has to do with the healing power of fairy tales.

Fairy tales which are useful in the psychotherapeutic process in helping the patient and his therapist to understand more about what went wrong, and why the patient reacts as he does, will not necessarily have any healing influence on the patient. Some fairy tales show the way in the diagnostic process. They help to find the areas of conflict and they help the patient to look at them in a new way. Other fairy tales seem to have more direct psychotherapeutic value. A particular fairy tale can be a diagnostic help to one patient and have healing qualities for another. This depends on the individual patient, his problems and the situation. If the right moment is chosen, one can sometimes get a clear view of important conflicts when asking the patient which fairy tale he dislikes most and why this is so.

Fairy tales deal with objects and actions, not so much with feelings. In a sense, feelings and emotions become expressed through individuals, objects and actions. Many people can share the symbolic world in fairy tales. Children don't interpret symbols, they experience things more directly and intuitively. The symbols, however, have their influence on the unconscious and appeal to basic drives. The witch may symbolize aspects of what the child hates or fears about its mother. It is a relief, which does not become burdened by guilt feelings, to wish that the witch would die. The dangerous dragon may represent negative feelings towards the father, and it is not dangerous to wish that the dragon also should disappear. The good fairy and the wise king may symbolize what the child loves in his parents (see Lundgren and Norrby 1988).

Sometimes there is a disturbed balance in our drive-satisfaction. Some basic drives do not become satisfied and when choosing fairy tales for psychotherapy it can be important to analyze this disturbance or lack of balance.

I shall therefore refer to a simplified model, which could be helpful when analyzing the individual person's problems in relation to fairy tale therapy. The drives that I have found it important to work with are the instinct of self preservation, the libidinous drives, the intellectual drives and the spiritual drives (see Chapter 1).

Sometimes a patient, realizing that fairy tales can be integrated in the psychotherapeutic process, will indicate a fairy tale which is important for him, perhaps because he likes it, perhaps because it illustrates his personal development or his life situation as he sees it. By drawing attention to a story, he will tell you something important about himself, because it happens within the psychotherapeutic atmosphere.

For some time, I had been seeing a female patient who was feeling lonely, depressed, living a very isolated life, apparently not able to change anything. Her life had not always been like that; there had been periods where she could laugh and where she had enjoyed living, but it was very long ago. Often she felt humiliated. Even if she knew in some part of herself that she was wise and had an understanding of many things, she expressed the idea that no one really showed her respect. Being a psychiatric patient made everything hopeless, since one could always say that she was crazy if one did not like her ideas.

One day, when we had finished our session and she was on her way out, she commented on a fairy tale book lying on my table. To talk about the psychotherapeutic room and the impact the room can have on a patient would be to open another big theme. We will not do this now, but, within this context, I had found that it was all right to have the small book within reach, well aware that it could attract attention and produce reactions from people coming in. So I said to her that sometimes fairy tales could be helpful. She then asked, if I knew *The Teapot* by Hans Christian Andersen, and when I said I only vaguely remembered it, she continued 'You should read it' (Andersen 1966, vol.4).

The teapot is a very short story starting as follows: 'There was a proud teapot, proud of its porcelain, proud of its long spout, proud of its broad handle. It had something in front, something behind, the spout in front and the handle behind, and that is what it liked to talk about. It never talked about its lid, for it was cracked, that was riveted, the lid had a defect, and we don't care to talk about our defects, others will see to that. The teapot was well aware of its qualities and also of the cracked lid, in the confident days of its youth. One day it was lifted by the most delicate hand, but the most delicate hand was clumsy, and the teapot was dropped.' Later in the story, it says 'It was a hard blow that it got, and yet the hardest blow was the way they laughed, they laughed at the teapot, and not at the clumsy hand.'

I read the story that I had not thought of for many years. It seemed quite clear that it could illustrate this woman's sorrow and pain. Not only had she been deeply hurt, but she had also felt ridiculed and humiliated, and nobody had apparently understood that the delicate hand taking care of her was clumsy. She had probably felt that Andersen had told her story through the teapot, and she made me see it as well. By calling my attention to the lovely teapot with the cracked lid dropped by a delicate, but clumsy hand, she had given a picture, which explained an enormous amount. This was important. When I mentioned the teapot, having read it, she called my attention to the fact that even if the broken teapot is thrown out at the end of the story, it does not completely lose its dignity and sense of value; perhaps this was what she really wanted to say.

Fairy tales can illustrate developmental stages in human life; thus we may prefer a particular fairy tale when we are eight and a different one when we are fourteen. As adults, we will look back on periods of our childhood, good times and bad times. Working with difficult periods in psychotherapy, the fairy tale, if one is included, would naturally be linked to the developmental period that is being worked with. If you as a psychotherapist introduce a fairy tale, it will be done based on knowledge, but intuition has to be there as well to give dynamic significance, and one must consider what psychological age is important when one chooses to work with a fairy tale or the symbols in the story.

When I see a patient for the first time, I often try to tune into his psychological age on that very day. The psychological age is different from the biological age, and it may change from one day to another. I find it important, because it gives one a feeling of where one is and where to start. Once I saw a man in his thirties in a closed ward. He was psychotic, very anxious and tense. He talked fast, and it was very difficult to follow him. We had to go through a psychological examination. My feeling was that his psychological age was somewhere between eight and eleven, corresponding to the latency age. When he was working with a psychological test (*Julian Rotter's Sentence Completion Test*) he wrote: 'As a child I was eight years'. No doubt eight years had been a very important stage in his life. When I asked him what happened at that stage he said 'I was taken to an infant's home, and my mother committed suicide'. He then mentioned the year his mother died. Then he must have been 19, but he obviously felt that he had lost her when he was eight. I only saw him for a few days. If it had been the beginning of psychotherapy, I would have had eight years in mind, and this age would be important in relation to choosing fairy tales.

Different Methods or Techniques of Using Fairy Tales in Psychotherapy

There are many ways in which one can use fairy tales. A fairy tale may have significance in your work with a patient, even if one never talks about it. This can be the case if one makes associations with a particular story, which ome does not choose to bring up. In this situation, the fairy tale may help the therapist become aware of certain conflicts. It may also create hope in him for the patient. One might say that, for the patient to gain hope, it is important for him to feel it in the therapist. As one patient expressed it, talking about a doctor she had been in contact with: 'I did not have any hope, but she had the hope for me'.

Bettelheim has written: 'By telling fairy tales to his child, a parent gives the child an important demonstration that he or she considers the child's inner experiences as embodied in fairy tales worthwhile, legitimate, in some fashion even "real". This gives the child the feeling that, since his inner experiences have been understood by the parent as real and important, he, by implication, is real and important.' Dealing with psychotic ideas, hallucinations and delusions within a fairy tale frame of reference, one will have the chance to give the experience of being understood to the patient, having made the patient see that the therapist is willing to share some of his inner experiences, if he will allow it.

Dreams and fantasies in mentally ill persons can be frightening, not only to the patient, but sometimes also to the professionals working with them. In working with forensic psychiatric patients there are acts which it may be difficult to face. In these situations it is important to keep in touch with one's own unconscious life as it manifests itself in dreams and fantasies. In a paradoxical way, a fairy tale frame of reference can help the therapist keep his own reality-orientation while being sensitive to his own fantasies and feelings and to the patient's feelings. One has to take part in the patient's inner drama, related to a drama in reality. It is, however, important not to become so absorbed in it as to lose the way.

Fairy stories speak to the conscious and the unconscious mind and do not need to avoid contradictions, since these easily coexist in our unconscious mind. This somehow explains extremely well the essential reason why these stories can be of great help in the treatment of neurotic persons who are afraid to be confronted with fantasies and wishes that are unacceptable to them. They are useful also in crisis intervention, when people can see no way out and search for a small light by which to orient themselves; and they are helpful in the treatment of psychotic people – a strange imaginary world manifests itself not only in the psychotic ideas and delusions, but also in the fairy tales.

Fairy tales have a message, which means that there is a kind of road to follow when reading the story. Many fairy tales have the same kind of beginning 'Once upon a time' and an ending like 'And they lived happily ever after, and if they have not died, they are living yet.' To a child this is a reassuring context, and so it is for the patient and his psychotherapist.

For some time I had been working with a young psychotic woman (I shall call her Kirsty). She had committed a serious crime and had therefore to stay in the hospital for a long time. She had talked much about her delusive ideas and the voices which had forced her to commit the crime. The voices came from an old woman, whom she had seen apparently only a few times. In her imagination, this woman had a strong negative and punishing influence on her, almost like a witch. During Kirsty's childhood she had had a very disturbed relationship with her mother, and the mother herself had had a difficult and traumatic childhood. Kirsty had expressed the wish to talk to me, but, as one would expect, she was suspicious, frightened, and sometimes angry. She was not sure that I wished to help and not harm her. Her life had never given her the experience that one can trust other people.

As psychotherapists, we try to create an atmosphere which provides space for another person to develop confidence; we do not always focus on the necessary changes in ourselves. Here, however, I had an intuitive feeling that a change in our relationship had to start in me, but how this was to happen I did not know. One day she told me that she had made a drawing which showed a girl standing on a leaf, and she described the dress which the girl was wearing.

I got the impression that the leaf was somehow flying in the air, not lying on the ground or growing on a tree. I then asked her about the leaf. She explained that the leaf was not lying on anything, so my immediate impression seemed to follow her idea, which is a reassuring feeling. I remembered an illustration by the Swedish artist Elsa Beskov, who has illustrated the fairy tale *Thumbelina* by Hans Christian Andersen (1979). Thumbelina is standing on a leaf that is floating on water, so I said to the patient: 'It is like *Thumbelina*'. She said she had not thought of *Thumbelina*, and later I found out that she knew the fairy tale, but not Elsa Beskov's illustration.

Shortly after this, she showed me her picture and I still thought that the mood was very much like *Thumbelina*. It was of a small girl with hair that was exactly the same colour as Kirsty's hair. In her drawing I saw a four-year-old girl standing on a leaf. The leaf was just in the air, her arms stretching towards a big sun, which was almost too close to the little girl. The body was that of a little girl, whereas the face seemed much older. It was in profile. It was not quite clear which way it was turning. Most of the face had been covered by the hair. The eye, as I saw it, had a curious expression, and the mouth was sceptical. Her facial expression illustrated conflicting, ambivalent feelings (her eyes received impressions, which her mouth seemed to repel). The girl's dress was blue, covered with flowers like small stars.

I could not see which way the girl was moving, whether she was coming or going. It was as if she was stretching her arms out towards the sun, but whether she was approaching the sun or sliding back from it, I could not see. I thought that this small figure floating in the atmosphere was something to go by. *Thumbelina* was the fairy tale which might somehow give me an emotional understanding, even if we never talked about Hans Christian Andersen's fairy tale. Much later, she told that she was about four years old when she felt threatened by a woman. The woman might very well have been real, but later she was part of her paranoid ideas.

Thumbelina starts: 'There was once a woman who did so want to have a wee child of her own, but she had no idea where she was to get it from. So she went off to an old witch and said to her: "I would so dearly like to have a little child. Do please tell me where I can find one." The witch gives a barleycorn to the woman, and the woman plants it and a lovely great flower comes up. "It is a pretty flower," said the woman, and she gave the lovely red and yellow petals a kiss, but directly she kissed it, the flower burst open with a pop. It was a real tulip – that was plain enough now – but, sitting on the green pistil in the middle of the flower, was a tiny little girl' (Andersen 1966 vol.1).

You probably remember that a great ugly slimy toad snatched Thumbelina out of her walnut-shell while she was asleep, because she would make a nice wife for her son. During the winter Thumbelina finds shelter in the field-mouse's home: 'You poor mite, said the field-mouse, for at heart she was a kind old thing.' The field-mouse gets the idea that Thumbelina should marry her neighbour, who is a mole. With the witch, the mother, the toad and the field-mouse, there is a feminine universe to start with. Thumbelina is snatched out of her bed, so one might say that her mother did not look after her and protect her, and she was threatened by a toad, who would give her to her son.

Kirsty never had a mother who could look after her and protect her from harm. She had wandered in the world on her own. She had good experiences as a child just like Thumbelina, but she had also been in great danger and had felt terribly lonely and frightened. When I saw her as a four-year-old Thumbeli-na on a green leaf in the air all alone moving nowhere or anywhere, I began to see where I could meet her. Our relationship changed; she started to work.

Many months later, our working alliance was threatened. This was at a time when her angry feelings and despair came out against me, and she let me know that I should no longer come to see her. I then thought of Thumbelina, who somehow seemed to have helped us to start with. I did not mention Thumbelina, since this would not be helpful to her as I saw it. I just hoped that there was still some confidence in her, even if it would not take up more room than a tiny Thumbelina.

When this critical phase was over, she showed me a drawing she had made of Thumbelina in a tulip, stretching her arms towards the sun. It was a Thum-belina, she said, who was afraid, almost in panic (to me she looked angry as well, and she looked very much like a boy). Her comment was: 'She cannot bear to be a girl, since so many frightful things have happened.' We could now talk about the desperate Thumbelina, the angry and lonely little girl who did not want to be a girl.

What was communicated from the beginning by my introduction of Thum-belina was an acceptance of Kirsty as a person explained through a symbol, a concrete picture. This picture was easier to deal with than more direct express-ions of feelings, which she might have rejected, not finding them trustworthy and too difficult to deal with.

When focusing attention on the psychoanalytically-oriented interpretation of fairy tales in psychotherapeutic work, different approaches to the same story will be found. In Little Red Riding Hood, meets interpretations which focus on oral greediness, aggression and sexual wants in the work of Bruno Bettelheim and other interpretations such as that of Vibeke Arndal (1985). Here we see Little Red Riding Hood as an illustration of the destructive power in the female universe. Relating to different versions of the fairy tale, interpreters put the emphasis on different aspects of the story, as illustrated very elegantly by Ole Vedfelt (Holbek 1987).

This is also the case when applying the fairy tale in psychotherapy – as has been pointed out by Verena Kast (1989). She uses Little Red Riding Hood as an example of a favourite tale that also arouses considerable anxiety or panic (angstmärchen). If the story is seen from the perspective of a feminine universe as an illustration of the destructive, devouring mother, the therapist's work will be very different from what happens if the story is seen from the perspective of an oedipal crisis.

There is no single correct interpretation of a dream, and just in the same way there is no single correct interpretation of a fairy tale. However, it is possible to work with the structure, symbols and actual story in a systematic way to gain one's own understanding and, when applying the fairy tale in psychotherapy, listen to the patient's experiences and associations, and see where they will take one. I have found four attitudes or techniques valuable in fairy tale therapy. These are:

1. The naive and intuitive approach.

2. Psychodynamic interpretation of symbols and themes in fairy tales.

3. The use of fairy tales as a kind of play-therapy.

4. Creating fairy tales.

The Naive Approach

The first and basic attitude I have called the naive approach, in which the patient gets into contact with the fairy tale in an intuitive and spontaneous way. It implies a close identification and an opportunity for the person to externalize what goes on in his mind in controllable ways. What Bettelheim (1976) has described in relation to children could just as well be applied to adults, who are in close contact with the child in themselves: 'The child can embody his destructive wishes in one figure, gain deserved satisfaction from another, identify with a third as his needs require' (p.65–66).

The naive approach is the primary characteristic of the small child between the age of one and a half and four years, the period described as the magic years by the child psychologist Selma H. Fraiberg (1973). She has written about the importance of dreams and fantasies in the first years of life and tried to explain the difficulty in childhood of learning the significance of language. One of her illustrative examples concerns a small boy, David, who was two and a half years old. He was going for a trip to Europe with his parents. They were talking about all the exciting things which were going to happen, starting with the long flight to Europe. After some time, David stopped asking questions and seemed distressed. One day he revealed his secret worry and said: 'I cannot go, since I cannot fly yet.' He had seen aeroplanes, but perhaps he did not know that people could be transported in them. He may have looked upon them as a kind of bird. Although this small boy was very good at communicating, he did not understand the difficult language he was presented with. The concrete meaning of a word will stay in our brains and attack our reason now and then. In childhood, the double meaning of words can be difficult, and in the life of the psychotic person it seems to be hard as well.

Fraiberg uses the expression 'weak words', meaning that the words are not yet organized in a way which allows for the possibility of continual memory. Magic thinking is particularly characteristic of the second year of life and of the adult psychotic person, it should be pointed out. It is during the first years of life that we experience fairy tales in a naive and spontaneous way. As small children we will hear many 'weak words'.

Sometimes we keep the naive approach to a fairy tale as a precious memory, like the young woman who was asked to give her associations with the tigers melting into butter in *Little Black Sambo*. In spite of the young woman's interest in the interpretation of literature, her answer was: 'No, I do not want to touch Little Black Sambo, I want to keep my naive and childish attitude to him with grandfather's voice in the back of my head.' It appeared that *Little Black Sambo* was the first fairy tale she remembered. It was closely associated with the cosy and comforting atmosphere she had experienced when sitting close to grandfather, listening to his voice, and the melody in the story that becomes clear through the many repetitions of the same phrases. The music created by grandfather's tone of voice, the pictures in the book, painted by the author Helen Bannerman (1900), were there as an entity, something precious which she could still recall for her inner ear and eye. With it were also memories of grandfather's face and his big soft hands when turning the pages in the book slowly and carefully. So many things happened in exactly the same way each time she asked to hear *Little Black Sambo*. And like so many children, she learned the story by heart. She knew the words by heart and should grandfather happen to skip a word or a sentence, she would be quick to correct him.

In this way, the situation gave her a feeling of something stable which could be foreseen in an otherwise changeable world. Grandfather was there to share experiences with her and to answer her questions, if she felt like asking any. She had the chance to influence her world. She could stop him and make a pause, dwell on a particular passage or picture and hold on to his hand turning the pages. In this way the fairy tale situation was quite different from watching a film on television, where the child has no influence on what is going on.

Rhymes and magic formulae in fairy tales are often repeated and they have a melodic quality which is reinforced by the reader. They may stay in the back of our head many years after we have listened to the story. Recalling a tone of voice from childhood sometimes brings the adult into contact with memories of important experiences in early childhood. Some fairy tales are illustrated, and the pictures become almost part of the story. Children have also created their own images, which have been part of their inner world through many years. They have helped them keep in contact with the child which is there, somewhere, in all of us.

The situation in which the fairy tale was told is important. Thus good childhood memories about fairy tales may include the memory of a cozy room, sitting close to an older person, perhaps eating something good, watching the fire, listening to the storm outside and even the smell in the air from warm chocolate or whatever it might be. It all becomes part of good memories. So very different from what one small girl experienced, when she had a fairy tale read to her as a reward when she was sexually abused for a long period by an elderly man. In psychotherapy many years later, she expressed an interest in fairy tales, in which a hiding-theme was important. If only she had had a big clock or something else to crawl into as a child, she might not have been abused.

The essence of the naive approach is that there is no attempt at direct interpretation, either from the patient or from the therapist. One might talk about sharing an experience, which is sometimes also sharing memories, if both know the story. There is a guiding thread in the choice of fairy tale, no matter whether the patient or the therapist brings it up.

A young woman called Susan had been in the hospital for ten years when a male psychologist saw her. In his attempt to get into contact with her, which was at that time fairly difficult, he asked her if there was any book she liked. She mentioned *Ronja Robberdaughter* by the Swedish author Astrid Lindgren (in English, *The Robber's Daughter* 1984). (I quote from the English translation of the book, but keep the original Swedish names.)

The story begins with the following words: 'The night when Ronja was born, a thunderstorm was raging over the mountains, such a storm that all the goblinfolk in Mattis' Forest crept back in terror to their holes and hiding-places. Only the fierce harpies preferred stormy weather to any other and flew, shrieking and hooting round the robber's stronghold on Mattis' mountain. This was painful to Lovis, who was lying there to give birth to her child, so she asked Mattis to chase them. Mattis tried to shoot at the harpies, and he cried that he was going to have a baby that night. "Hoho, he is going to have a baby to night", hooted the harpies "a thunder-and-lightning baby, small and ugly it'll be ho, ho."'

In Alan Dundes book of (1982) scenes similar to the opening scene in *Ronja Robberdaughter* have been characterized in the following way: 'A terrible slaughter always takes place at the time of the birth of the hero, as for instance the killing of the infants at Bethlehem, when Christ was born.' As for the psychologist, he saw the drama of birth also as an emotional drama, and some of its aspects might give associations to the beginning of a psychosis.

We shall not go into detail with this story, just emphasize that it illustrates the difficult process of loosening emotional bonds between a daughter and her father. Two groups of robbers live in the mountain, they fight each other, and during the frightful night the mountain is split into two halves. The two children – the girl Ronja and the boy Birk – belonging to the two families fighting each other, become separated. They are on each side of the huge cliff, almost a picture of the dramatic split of the androgynous existence explained in the chapter on Peter Pan. Ronja grows up, and she leaves her home and her father before reaching puberty. He reacts very strongly to this, and for a very long time he will not recognize her as his daughter. To grow up and become independent, she has to be lonely and on her own for quite some time.

Being alone without much support from her family was also what had happened to Susan. Talking about Ronja and the other figures in the story produced continuity in the contact with this young woman and her therapist. Even if he never interpreted the story with words, it seemed to help her in her gradual identity development. In a way, one might say both found confidence with the story as a mutual field of experience. Much was well known to both of them, but with good stories there is always something new to find and share.

Gradually, she began to understand the essence of psychotherapeutic communication, even if their contact could not be called psychotherapy in a strict sense. For a long period, it was a question of establishing a relationship and helping her break through her isolation from the world around her. She never left the ward on her own. Part of the development was for the therapist to encourage her to leave the ward for a short while, at first with him.

One day the two of them were going for a walk, and when she talked about the birds, he said: 'The birds fly freely about;' she commented: 'But I am not free, I am not free.' She obviously had the feeling that when he talked about the birds, he wanted to say something which was important to her, something that included more than the birds, and she responded to this. She responded to the metaphor and seemed to be near a time for psychotherapy.

The therapist found he got a new understanding of the young female patient through his own work with the fairy tale and it was helpful to him. What happened to her in relation to the fairy tale, we do not know, because together they stayed within the spontaneous or naive approach, but like Ronja who had the courage to leave her home and be on her own, Susan gradually moved away from the ward on her own. They talked about frightening harpies in Ronja's life, when she went out into the woods, and gradually the frightening creatures in Susan's inner world became less dangerous.

It is probably important to emphasize that sharing the fairy tale with the patient without any attempt to start an interpretative process sometimes seems to be the best thing the psychotherapist can do. At the same time, the naive approach does not exclude psychoanalytically-oriented therapy and thus integration on a higher level at a later period. The following case illustrates this. The focus of attention, from the therpist's point of view, seemed to be a concern for the patient's tone of voice.

In his psychoanalytic paper 'Beyond Semantics' the Norwegian psychoanalyst Bjørn Killingmo (1990) describes the psychoanalytic process with a young woman in her late twenties who was a translator and yet had great difficulties in expressing her emotions in words. She felt her value as a person was decided by others and even if this evaluation was usually likely to be a positive one, it was not enough to make her feel valuable as a person. Her speech was high and unmodulated. She never used expressions such as 'I feel,' or referred to emotions such as anger, sorrow, jealousy; she seemed afraid to use words freely.

In one of the first sessions, she came up with a theme which gradually became a key to the understanding of her identity-development. She had always liked an old Norwegian folk-song from The Telemark about the young daughter of a farmer. As she passes the steep mountain on her way to church, a troll comes out, enticing her to pay him a visit. Inside the mountain the troll closes the door and she is forbidden to leave. She has to marry the troll and give birth to his children. Only once, after many years, is she allowed to pay a visit to her old parents, but she has to keep her promise to the troll and return to the mountain, where she is left to end her days. It is even told that she was not allowed to be buried in Christian soil. So she was expelled from mankind. The refrain of the ballad reads as follows: 'Time seems to drag – I alone bear the confinement of mourning.'

Killingmo had the feeling that the young woman would not really let him in; she kept her inner imaginary world very much to herself, and when he called her attention to that, she answered: 'It is not merely a question of moving in as a guest. You have to give up something at the door.' The author thought that humanity has to be given up when living with the troll, and he calls attention to the fact that the same theme appears in Ibsen's *Per Gynt*. In order to see the troll's eyes, Per has to slash one of his own eyes. However, by doing so he will be for ever isolated from the world of human beings.

As for this woman, it was difficult for her to create a connection between words and feelings – between her inner and outer world. She had a very controlling mother, and from being a lively and spontaneous child she had changed into a very nice and well behaved girl. In her fantasy, she developed the idea of being a 'hulder' a half-human and half-creature from the underworld, not granted full privileges in the world of human beings. A hulder is a supernatural female creature from Norwegian folktales with a cow's tail. She is very beautiful and lives inside mountains and hills. This young woman was living a double life, keeping her inner world a secret.

In her she had acoustic memory traces, and Killingmo got the feeling that she had sensed her mother's anxiety as a small girl in the intonation in her voice. To reach this patient in therapy, the tone of voice became very important, and while listening to the therapist, it was as if she was always listening to her mother. The sound space has a great impact on the small child, and the world becomes disturbing if the mother's voice communicates neither what the child feels nor what she feels about the child.

What appeared helpful in the psychotherapeutic situation was the speech sound. When an experiential link had been established with her early potential, the retreat into fantasy and identifications with figures and themes from fairy tales and folklore became accessible to analysis. Before an actual interpretation was possible, attention was drawn to the acoustic qualities in the fairy tale and thus to something very basic.

Some years ago a schizophrenic patient said that he had heard his therapist reading a paper on the radio, and he thought it was good, so she asked him what he liked about it, and he answered 'your tone of voice'. He did not seem to care about the content, or at least he would not say anything about it, but the tone of voice was important. Another day he said to his therapist that when he was frightened, he tried to remember her voice.

The fairy tale interpreter and psychoanalyst Katrin Asper has described what she calls the classic Jungian method, which implies that a person gets into a dialogue with his inner figures and thus gets into contact with them. Jung calls this method active imagination. It is a dialogue with the unconscious, in which inner figures acquire independent life; they may have different attitudes from the ego, but this is accepted and thus there seems to be a way out of the conflict or a way to solve the conflict. All the figures in our dreams are part of our inner personality, and the figures in fairy tales could be looked upon in the same way. Sometimes they are easier to work with than dreams, because they are not as private as dreams.

Through the rhythms in songs and folk stories it seems possible to gain access to the acoustic space from very early childhood and thus to basic and archaic feelings. This is also what I would call part of the naive approach to fairy tales in childhood and in psychotherapy with adults. It is often the case with children that they want to hear the same story again and again, and sometimes they ask you to read the same passages several times. When this happens, it is probably because the illustrated motives have significance for the child, just as we see it in the repetition of dreams. In this situation it is important to be attentive and find out what the child is concerned about.

Marianne Runberg describes children who were emotionally deprived as small children and who found confidence and hope in particular fairy tales read by an adult, who could understand what it was about and communicate an understanding with the child, without talking about the traumatic experiences. For this the child had no words, since they took place in an early period of life, when the child had not mastered language. How can you expect a child to talk about anxiety, despair, anger and sorrow when it was parted from its mother at the age of one?

A girl of eight was the smaller of two sisters. For some time she had been preoccupied with thoughts about whether her parents, particularly her father, would have preferred to have had a boy instead of a girl when she was born. At this time she heard the story of *Peter Pan* and her favourite passage was the scene in which Peter Pan tells Wendy that one girl is worth more than ten boys. This happens when Wendy has sewn his shadow to his heel. In the beginning he is just very satisfied with himself, completely forgetting that it was Wendy who did the sewing, but when she calls his attention to the fact that she was the one who did it, he comes out with this fabulous praise.

When the girl's mother saw her reaction to Peter's respect for Wendy and other girls, she became aware of her daughter's thoughts, which she had not been before, even if the girl had expressed them quite clearly. She became aware of the importance of confirming her daughter's self-confidence and of supporting her feminine identity, and she was able to make the father understand how important it was for his daughter to feel accepted not only as a child, but

P

---

*   *The story has many similarities with **Cinderella** and is retold in **Cinderella: A Folklore Casebook** by Alan Dundes (1982), in which von Franz gives her interpretation of the story.*

articularly as a daughter.

Psychodynamic Interpretation of Symbols and Themes in Fairy Tales; Transitional Objects in Fairy Tales

In a psychoanalytically oriented analysis of the Russian fairy tale *Wassilissa the Beautiful,* Hirsch and Hirsch-Löwer (1986) describe the developmental process from dependence in the very early mother-child relationship to liberation and self realization in adulthood.*

One of the important figures in the story is a doll which, according to the authors, is given the role of a transitional object in the sense described by Winnicott. This means that the doll acts as a helper and guide for Wassilissa, who has to live with a wicked stepmother and two evil step-sisters. In the fairy tale we are confronted as readers with many aspects of the mother-figure, such as the good, loving mother, the wicked stepmother, the witch and the wise old lady.

The fairy tale contains the comforting message for the small child (as well as for the adult) that he or she is not the only one with anxiety and conflicts, and there are suggestions for possible ways of solving conflicts. There is a purpose in the fairy tale, signalling to the child that it should give up childish wishes to be dependent and have the courage to live an independent life.

The atmosphere is very well illustrated by the first few lines: 'In the land of the Tzar, behind the blue seas and behind the tall mountains, a merchant was living with his wife. They had an only daughter, and she was so pretty that everybody called her Beautiful Wassilissa. When the child was eight years old, the wife suddenly became ill. She called Wassilissa to her deathbed, gave her a doll, and said, "Listen, my dear child, these are my last words and don't forget them. I am dying and give you my blessings and this doll. Keep it always with you, show it to nobody, and whenever you are in any trouble ask it for advice." Then she kissed her daughter for the last time and died.'

As you have already guessed, the merchant marries a widow and thus gains two step-daughters. The stepmother is jealous of Wassilissa because of her beauty and makes her work very hard. In the story about Wassilissa she is sent out into the woods by the stepmother to meet Baba Yaga. Baba Yaga is a witch and the place where she lives has animal characteristics; her hut stands on chicken's legs and dog's feet. On her way to Baba Yaga, Wassilissa meets three men on horseback. The three male figures represent a dynamic aspect of the Great Mother, perhaps a certain masculine ruthlessness going along with the maternal principle, or the active, dynamic side of the unconscious (according to von Franz). All the way through she is given help by the doll, but she also takes care of the doll. Meeting Baba Yaga does not become a destructive process, because she is protected by the doll, which she feeds well. The doll can be looked upon as a transitional object, representing the good mother (Hirsch and Hirsch-Löwer 1986).

Separation anxiety is an important aspect in this fairy tale, and just as the small child seeks comfort from its teddy bear when mother is leaving, Wassilissa seeks help in her doll. Working with a young woman who coped very well in her intellectual life, but had emotional difficulties, we got to a stage where it seemed important for her to make some changes in her private life in order to gain emotional maturity and independence.

It was my feeling that it would be important for her to break up some relationships and be on her own for some time. However, she could not make this decision. One of the reasons might be that it created separation anxiety, which might be a repetition of an anxiety she had felt as a very small child in her relationship with her mother, at an age at which she could not yet speak.

Hubback (1990) has pointed at other possible explanations. 'It can also happen that when someone in analysis is resisting change, the resistance may be an indication that he has introjected the anxiety that will be caused to others in his environment if he does not consider them, but that he is unconscious of that introjection' (p.114). As well as this, Hubback points out the fact that the reason why there is no change has to be found in the therapist. 'If we become anxious about no change, we have to watch out for unconscious manipulations on our part designed to bring about what we want. In that case, it is the analyst who needs to change before the patient can' (p.115).

The time perspective, the feeling that a change was significant, was reinforced by a dream the patient had, in which something important was to happen before the clock struck twelve – very much a fairy tale theme. Still keeping the time perspective in mind, I reached a stage at which I realized that, by being so concerned about the theme of change, I might be reinforcing her anxiety. So I tried to keep this in mind which, as I see it now, was helpful. One day I came across the fairy tale about Wassilissa.

In the story the stepmother sends Wassilissa out into the woods. Going into the woods could show introspective work and a readiness to get in touch with the unconscious. I gave the fairy tale to the young woman and suggested to her that she should read it and see if it could be of any help. I told her that I might be wrong, but I just thought there was a possibility that she could use it.

She read the fairy tale, but did not get much out of it. So we decided to leave it at that. After some time, she went on a holiday and when she came back, she told me that she had taken the fairy tale with her. It had been a comforting feeling just to have it with her. One could say that the paper had got the quality of a transitional object in itself. How could that be? We discovered that one reason might be that I had written her name on it. Hearing one's own name or, sometimes, reading it, can support good feelings about personal identity and integrity.

She had read the story again, and now she got the feeling of what it was about. She did make some decisive changes in her life, and she went through a period which required courage, concentration and somehow also isolation. It seemed the fairy tale had been important to her at a particular stage, when she was ready to read it. I came to her too early with the story, but she had been able to wait until the right moment. The story given to her was written in the language she had spoken as a child, which was not Danish, and thus not the language she and I were speaking together. Having heard the story in her mother tongue had probably helped her to get in touch with her emotions, when the right moment came.

At the beginning, she looked upon Wassilissa as the passive girl waiting for the prince, a feminine role she could not identify with. Gradually, she became able to integrate different aspects of the feminine character in the fairy tale and in real life as well. She came to realise, somehow, that she was not only princess, but also prince in her own life story.

When a patient approaches the time of termination in psychotherapy one has to say goodbye, and this is often difficult, causing separation anxiety and reviving sorrow from earlier losses in life. The idea of psychotherapy is to help the patient integrate what he or she has been working through in psychotherapy, until one day therapy is no longer needed. If therapy has been helpful, the patient will not forget his therapist, who will not forget his patient either. The therapist will always be there, somehow resting on a nearby cushion, like Wassilissa's doll, having finished its work. In this way, the fairy tale may also have a reassuring influence. (In the chapter on *Peter Pan* I have tried to illustrate the use of a fairy tale within psychoanalytically oriented psychotherapy in more detail.)

Fairy Tales as Play Therapy
It is also possible to use fairy tales as a kind of play therapy, in which the patient is allowed to identify with fairy tale figures and to live or relive passages of his own life through the figures. In the same way, fairy tales help him to understand important aspects of the emotional relationships between the child and important persons in his life, such as parents, siblings, and friends. This is what we have tried to illustrate in the chapter *Pinocchio as a Helper in Psychotherapy*.

Creating a Fairy Tale
Another way of working with fairy tales is for the individual to make his or her own story, either taking place in real life as a kind of self therapy, or as part of a psychotherapeutic process.

To create a fairy tale or tell a story can be a helpful process. This is illustrated by Marianne Runberg in the chapter on child development, in which the six-year-old boy, having been taken away from his parents and in coping with the adaptation to his new family, makes up a story about a kitten that left its parents, but was taken care of by two horses. In this chapter there is also a description of a girl of thirteen struggling with the beginnings of separation from her parents as she starts the developmental phase of puberty. She wrote the story *The Fairy Tale Wood*.

To create a fairy tale can also be a helpful process for an adult dealing with a life crisis; an illustrative example might be *Little Black Sambo* (Bannerman 1900). This extremely simple story was analyzed from a Freudian psychoanalytic point of view by Marjorie McDonald (1974), who also analysed the story in relation to the author's personality and her life.

Helen Bannerman, who was Scottish, was married to an army doctor stationed in India. In the mid 1930s she lived in Edinburgh. She was described as 'a small, quiet, gray-haired Scotchwoman with a kind face and what might be called a dignified twinkle in her eyes.' Those were the words of her American publisher, who visited her in her home, where she lived with one of the daughters for whom she wrote *Little Black Sambo*.

She was born in Edinburgh, daughter of an army chaplain who had been stationed in various corners of the Empire. His large family went with him, and when his daughter Helen was two years old they were sent to Madeira, where they remained for ten years. She married an army doctor as a young woman and thirty years of her married life were spent in India. It was in 1889, when she was returning to India leaving her two little girls at home in Scotland, that she wrote *The Story of Little Black Sambo*. She sent the story home to her children, but she also wrote it to comfort herself on the long railway-journey that took her away from them. According to Marjorie McDonald she wrote the story and illustrated it as a creative effort to master a most painful separation.

Sambo is outfitted in 'a beautiful red coat and a pair of beautiful little blue trousers'. He wears purple shoes with crimson soles and crimson linings and carries a beautiful green umbrella, both purchased specially for him by his father. Thus bedecked Sambo goes out for a walk all by himself into the jungle.

McDonald is of the opinion that the clothing made by the mother might represent the child's transitional objects, which enable it to endure the developmental separation from her. This could be compared with the doll in *Beautiful Wasilissa*. The father's gifts of coloured shoes and an umbrella symbolize the strength which the father passes on to his son.

The author chose a small boy as a hero instead of a girl. McDonald suggests that unconsciously she regarded a boy as better equipped to face the world on his own. In fairy tales it is often the hero who travels out into the world. The parents in the story are 'the right kind of parents, just the kind every child would like to have'. Sambo meets the three tigers, and he gives away all his fine clothes to the tigers so as not to be eaten up by them. 'And poor little Black Sambo went away crying, because the cruel tigers had taken all his fine clothes.'

The tigers start fighting while Sambo is looking on, standing behind a palm tree. This scene is interpreted as the primal scene: that is, parents' sexual intercourse witnessed by the child, which feels 'wee and far away,' lonely and excluded from this strange fight that is going on between its parents. It is important to emphasize that, in this interpretation, McDonald suggests that the primal scene that is behind the fighting tigers, so to speak, is created on an unconscious basis.

The melted butter, which is the culmination of the tigers' wild running around the tree, is used for Black Mumbo's pancakes, and they are seen as a symbol of little tigers issuing from the parents' fighting and again interpreted as the child's idea of oral conception, the idea that mother gets a baby in her tummy through eating, which makes her fat.

McDonald expresses the idea that Bannerman not only coped with separation from her own children, who were approaching school age, when writing *Little Black Sambo*, but also with separation conflicts from her own childhood, when she had had to leave Scotland as a very small girl of two years old.

It is interesting that Bannerman refused to write any more about Sambo for forty years. In 1936 she was visited by her publisher, who tried to persuade her to write another Sambo book. She insisted that she could not write more: 'You must remember that nearly forty years have passed. Little Black Sambo is a middle-aged gentleman now'. The publisher talked about his little girls, from whom he was separated, and how much they were longing for another Sambo book. Three weeks later, the book *Sambo and the Twins* was lying on his desk. McDonald thinks that the separation situation made her write again, since her letter to the publisher contained the following: 'You must remember that this is your own children's book. If it had not been for them I should never have written it at all.'

In the new Sambo book the twins are kidnapped by monkeys and poor Mumbo sat down and cried and cried and cried. Finally, a kind eagle rescues the children, and they all have pancakes. The theme of separation is central in this book.

Little Black Sambo is normally very appealing to the small child between the ages of two and three years, the years of magic thinking, where the child is dealing with separation anxiety and beginning oedipal conflicts. So, on the unconscious level, it appeals to the child's libidinous drives. This fairy tale is special in the sense that the author illustrated it herself, so the pictures in the book are very well integrated and add to its strong impact on children.

In small children's nightmares, wild animals play their part, and it is a comforting feeling that Sambo gains control over the tigers, since they melt away. By eating the tigers in the shape of melted butter as part of the pancakes one could also say that strength and aggression are integrated in a healthy way. In this way the tigers could be seen also as part of Sambo's own personality.

The story touches very basic, instinctive reactions in early life; this is probably also why the young woman did not want to have her memory of Little Black Sambo disturbed by trying to interpret the story. In the larger story about Sambo and his mother, Bannerman also provides an illustration of the significant sensitive periods in our lives. There are moments where we are able to be creative on the basis of inner and outer stimulations. In psychotherapy it is important to be aware of these moments of intensity in the patient's experience, to facilitate the process of growth. In ordinary life we also can be good fairies to other people and to ourselves, giving the small push at the right time or making room for expression to what seems ready to take form.

Concluding Remarks

Working with fairy tales, it has been encouraging to experience the interest that many staff members in the hospital showed in fairy tale interpretation, and this has given us something to share, which seemed to stimulate our fantasy, sense of humour and our concern for each other. Instead of focusing our attention on the pathological aspects of the patients' inner lives, their delusions, thought-disturbances and paranoid ideas, we could focus on some of the more healthy or creative aspects in thought disturbances, which we also find in fairy tales. No psychotic ideas are so crazy that one cannot find something similar in fairy tales.

CHAPTER 3

Fairy Tales in the Care and Treatment of Emotionally Deprived Children

Marianne Runberg

Introduction

This chapter deals primarily with the use of fairy tales in helping emotionally disturbed children. Help can be given by people involved with the children during their daily life – for example, foster parents.

My husband and I have worked with children in custody for many years. Confrontation with the severe disturbances in these children and the feelings of powerlessness they can give you made me interested in the story of 'our children' in particular; at the same, time I developed a wider interest in the general perspective of children living in custody.

It seemed characteristic that the anamnestic data available were often very meagre, and that the children's biological parents were frequently absent from their lives for long periods from the very beginning. The relationship with the mother had been disturbed with periods in which the child had lived separated from its mother, and there had been hardly any contact with her. Often, the child had been placed in several different children's homes or institutions. Many biological mothers had an alcohol problem.

When the child had been placed in a foster home or institution, there was often great uncertainty amongst authorities, biological parents and children themselves as to what was going to happen in the future. There was no long-term planning in most of the cases, and during the shifting, unstable periods no 'key-persons' providing continuity of help to these children.

In *Beyond the Interest of the Child* (Goldstein et al. 1973) there is an illustration of the importance of what is called 'psychological parents' in a child's life, whether these are biological parents, foster-parents or nursing-parents. In relation to the concept of psychological parents, what matters is a wholehearted wish to take care of the child on a practical and on an emotional level, giving the child the chance of a healthy personal and social development. This does not imply exclusively positive feelings, of course. The main thing will be that the positive feelings dominate, based on a daily contact with shared experiences.

This gives the child the chance to feel that it is a valuable member of the family. To achieve a satisfying relationship mutuality in the relationship between the child and its parents is of vital importance.

If the child's positive feelings for the 'parents' are not met with acceptance, the child will never really sense that it is loved and appreciated by at least one person. The child will not become able to love and respect itself, which again prevents it from taking care of others when growing up. One important thing is the need for a life which provides a feeling of continuity. This implies stability in family life, kindergarden, school, and so forth.

Emotional growth in childhood is never smooth. Sometimes growth may be fast, at other times one will find developmental arrest or even regression. To compensate for this internal lack of balance the child needs stability and harmony in the outer world. This need is sometimes overlooked by those taking care of the child living in a custodial setting.

The sense of time is important in relation to children placed in foster homes. The experience of time is very different to a child from that of a grown-up. The adult can normally make plans for the future, postponing the satisfaction of some of his or her needs, until the time is right to fulfil them. The child is not able to the same extent to wait for the satisfaction of its needs, and it is not able to plan for the distant future. What seems a fairly short time to the adult will be experienced as a very long time by the child, sometimes endless or 'forever' depending upon the child's biological age and developmental level. The time it takes to 'forget' an old emotional relationship and establish a new one will vary, depending upon the developmental stage of the child when the break took place (Goldstein et al. 1973).

Before the age of two years, it will be difficult for the child to hold on to an inner picture of the parents for very long. The child will become attached to new adults when the parents are not there, if these new adults meet the child's needs, and the child is not yet very disturbed. This, however, does not mean that the child continues life without an emotional scar because of the separation from its biological mother (and father, if he was ever there).

Reading fairy tales to a child seems to give some opportunities of compensating for what the child has been missing. The fairy tale may help to provide feelings of safety, predictability and continuity to the child. This happens within the situation of fairy tale reading, in which the child and the adult can have a quiet time together before bedtime. It is important to create a stable situation, in which many of the same things happen again and again. In this way, the child becomes able to foresee the situation. Life becomes safer, and the child gains the possibility of having a close and warm contact with one or two adults.

Apart from the reading situation, the fairy tale will communicate stability and safety to the child through the music and rhythm that frequently characterize fairy tales. In fairy tales time is not measured in days, months, and years, but in a certain number of trials. In this way the time perspective becomes easy to see, and possible for the child to understand.

Often the hero/heroine is unwanted, chased by evil persons/powers, but in the end the prince wins the princess, or the other way round. In this way, the hope to become a desired member of a family is communicated to the child, which feels rejected by its parents. As for the older children, it will sometimes on a symbolic level become 'acceptable' to feel attached to new people. The process is often difficult, since the children are burdened with guilt feelings, and they are afraid to be disloyal to their biological parents, even if the contact with these parents is very rare or no longer exists. The fairy tale is like a bond between the caring person and the child and a tool, by means of which the child can receive help in moving towards positive development.

You cannot ask a small child to tell you about its feelings during early childhood, what it was like to live away from home, perhaps without any connection with its parents. Most children, however, can refer to a favourite fairy tale and by finding this story and carefully identifying symbols which are important to the child, an understanding may be gained of the child's needs and feelings.

It is important to emphasize the distinction between fairy tale psychotherapy carried out by a professional psychotherapist, and guidance thorough fairy tales carried out by those who take care of the child. Supervision given to foster-parents dealing with disturbed children is sometimes a very good idea, but foster-parents should not become psychotherapists to their children.

Early Memories

Very early traumatic events may have taken place, before the deprived children had mastered language. Memories therefore exist on a preverbal level, which makes it difficult, perhaps even impossible for the person to talk about what happened. Moreover, one will frequently deal with events covered in taboos. The child needs to protect itself from a direct and clear confrontation, so one meets expressions of covered dream images. It is, however, sometimes possible for the child to recall vague images, sensations, moods around fairly early events, and the child may reveal a fascination for certain fairy tales or passages in fairy tales, which in one way or other seem to contain earlier experiences.

In psychotherapy one will often hear people describe early memories as dream-like pictures. They cannot be located precisely as belonging to reality or fantasy; perhaps one has to deal with a mixture of impressions from the outer and inner world. What is important in this situation is really the feeling and the mood contained in the memory.

The fairy tale is a good frame, within which one can 'safekeep' such early pictures and feelings. The fairy tale does not offer a finished or complete picture; although there can be many sharp details in fairy tales, there are also vague references such as 'once upon a time' or 'far far away behind the blue mountains'. The vague references create good opportunities for the protection of personal feelings and experiences.

To give space for the child's personal experiences, it seems a good idea to choose fairy tales which can be read or told without the use of illustrations. The child is then free to create inner pictures. If one reads or tells the story, the child may sometimes feel encouraged to take over and finish the story as and when it likes. Perhaps it will draw or paint its own illustrations.

A patient in psychotherapy, while listening to a passage in a story, made his own illustrations. The pictures showed the changes which the hero had to face. At the same time it was quite clear that the pictures showed his own difficulties, anxiety and confusion. The hero was in great danger. On this occasion the therapist chose to take some time concentrating on his drawing. She drew a lifebelt to rescue the hero in danger, and from the drawing she tried in words to create bonds to reality. From reality, she could take the patient back to the story again, and together they could move towards the good ending. When moving from one area to another, one has the opportunity to guide the patient through the story. The inner tension and feelings of anxiety do not become so overwhelming that it is unbearable. It is possible, for a short period, to approach the patient's problems, and on a realistic level set free some of his feelings, creating a balance again when returning to the story.

In the same way, a caring person will be able to give a child a 'lifebelt', if the child needs one when listening to a story. Perhaps one gives the lifebelt in words, perhaps through physical closeness in the contact between child and adult.

Fantasy and Reality
It is very important for the emotionally disturbed children to have a regular and stable daily rhythm, with structure and reliability. They seem to need clear boundaries to protect themselves from 'floating around'. It is characteristic that these children have a fragile reality-orientation. In many situations, where they feel frightened or uneasy, they will tend to use their imagination in a negative way. A child playing may misunderstand the reactions from its playmates, because it has difficulty in distinguishing between fantasy and reality. If there is no adult, who can interfere and create order, the situation may become difficult for the child to handle, or the child will panic, as was the case one day when an eight-year-old boy became absolutely terrified. His hair was full of chewing gum, which had to be removed with petrol. This made him afraid that his whole head would dissolve.

Another child may be heavily burdened with feelings of guilt. 'If only I had been a good girl, it would not have happened' (referring to the separation from her biological mother). In such a situation, it is also very important that the adult interferes and helps the child to get a realistic orientation.

It is characteristic that the best days for these children are ordinary days, – not Christmas Day or holidays, but a typical, ordinary 'grey' day, when the family will rise at a regular time, and bedtime is followed by a story with certain rituals carried out. Sitting in front of a video, in which fiction and reality come close to each other, seems to have a negative influence on these children.

Some modern science-fiction films seem to force imagination into a definite pseudo realistic pattern, and these don't help the child to expand its own inner world. In the fairy tale there is much more space; the child can take in what it needs, and the story is adaptable to the child's developmental level. A good story contains concrete and abstract values. The child can identify with fairy tale figures, and it is possible to sort out what is imagination and what is reality. This seems to be particularly important.

Structure and Symbols in Fairy Tales

Fairy tales may appeal to us on two levels. One level has to do with the immediate and spontaneous: good and evil forces fight each other and the good ones win. The hero functions as a model to imitate in the sense that the hero is a projection of the self helping the ego to develop. The immediate appearance has to do with the conscious ego, since the child will always identify with the hero.

The second level appeals to the unconscious by means of symbols richly represented in fairy tales. On the unconscious level the child will relate the symbols to its own inner conflicts. Gradually, the child may become aware of its conflicts and ready to accept help to work with them. Bettelheim (1976) explains this in the following way: 'Since all is expressed in symbolic language in fairy tales, the child can disregard what he is not ready for by responding only to what he has been told on the surface. But he is also enabled to peel off, layer by layer, some of the meaning hidden behind the symbol as he becomes gradually ready and able to master and profit from it' (p.279).

Time and place in fairy tales have eternal value because of their abstract character. The figures are very clearly described as either good or evil, and their behaviour does not change in an unpredictable way which could disturb the child. Another important aspect is their orientation towards the future, and the future is normally positive. 'While the fantasy is unreal, the good feelings it gives us about ourselves and our future are real, and these real good feelings are what we need to sustain us' (ibid p.126).

The fairy tale does not tell us about a happy solution being reached without any effort. The many different stories all tell us about a certain problem, which is not solved before the hero or heroine has been through trials and suffering. This means that the child does not come through its crisis until it is ready to develop through struggle, and until expanded recognition and maturity has been achieved.

The child becomes motivated through the fairy tale to do something itself, to be active. As expressed by Julius E. Heuscher in *Death in the Fairy-Tale* (1967) 'Growth means change. It may seem paradoxical that in order to strengthen our identity we must be willing to accept change, and that our identity wanes, if we try to strengthen it by avoiding any change within our make-up.'

The atmosphere in which the person develops during early childhood has unquestionably a profound effect upon the ways he later experiences change. When choosing fairy tales to support children, it does not seem to matter if the hero is not of the same sex as the child. A boy (like Jeff – see p.54) may thus identify with Snow White, since her problems have a general character. He can feel pleasure when the witch is punished, without simultaneously being burdened with feelings of guilt and get some relief from the stored anger towards his mother, who let him down. The mother, which you dare not hate on the conscious level, you may be able to punish on the unconscious level through symbols in fairy tales. The fairy tale gives the child the opportunity to express feelings of catharsis and thus relief from inner tension. One shows the child the possibility of repairing on a symbolic level what has been a bad mother-image, or at least one can help the child to attain a more faceted and positive mother-image by setting some negative feelings free.

Mother Images

Every child needs to have psychological parents, or at least one parent – either mother or father. Children placed outside their homes have frequently been without a father prior to this. The central conflicts have been concentrated on disturbances in relation to the mother or even separation from her. In the following we will look upon the mother's significance for the child's development or its developmental disturbance. This is not to minimize the significance of a good father or father figure.

Neumann (1976) emphasizes the fact that it is very important for the child to receive emotional care and love. He expresses the idea that if a child loses its mother during the period during which there is normally a primary mother-child relationship, the child will be emotionally deprived, and there is a danger that this will disturb the ego development and the instinct of self preservation (p.21). What is dangerous to the child, according to Neumann, is not so much whether the child's physical needs are looked after adequately, as whether the child experiences the feeling of loss of love and understanding, if the child loses the archetypal image of 'The Good Mother'.

By 'archetypal', Neumann means symbolic images in the unconscious. 'The Great Mother' implies positive and negative aspects. (The Good/Evil Mother ruling over life and death). In the normal mother-child relationship the child will experience an interaction between negative and positive actions, but with

a clear preponderance of the positive, which gives strength to overcome the more negative aspects without psychic harm to the child.

In the primary relationship between mother and child, the small child will normally experience the mother as 'The Good Strong Mother,' since she is the one who protects and gives nourishment. In this way the mother will develop the archetypal image of 'The Good Mother' in the child through her deeds. If, for some reason or other, the mother cannot behave as 'The Good Mother,' this will influence the child's mother image in a negative way, and in the unconscious it will develop pictures of the archetypal 'Evil Mother'.

The Good Mother does not have to be the child's biological mother; it can be another person taking care of the child, protecting and loving it. What seems important is apparently the presence of a particular person in the primary relationship, trying to understand and fulfil the needs of the child and giving the child a feeling of security. One might say that what the child needs is a person containing the archetypal features which characterize 'The Good Mother'. Any deviation from the archetypal features in the mother will affect the primary mother-child relationship. It will have a disturbing effect on the child's development in different degrees, depending upon how disturbed the relationship will be. Neumann thinks that a very disturbed primary mother-child relationship may lead to psychoses, particularly schizophrenia. In such a situation the child will have the experience that the world is falling apart, the end being near. Neumann has found that adults with this background may develop visions and dreams. These indicate that everything is dissolved in death and isolation; evil forces are fighting each other. The child will no longer experience the mother as 'The Good Mother,' reacting to the world in a positive way. The mother is then the 'The Evil Mother,' who can dissolve the world in which the child is living, but rather than this she creates chaos.

The archetypal symbols attached to 'The Evil Mother' are, among others, death, condemnation, drought, hunger and thirst. When the child experiences the mother manifesting herself as 'The Evil Mother,' it will no longer feel safe enough and have confidence enough to develop a stable ego, since ego formation depends upon the mother helping the child to incorporate those negative experiences which will eventually turn up during a developmental process. The Good Mother will try to satisfy the child's hunger, and she will relieve its fears. In this way the child learns to tolerate uncomfortable feelings, since it will receive help quickly. 'The Evil Mother,' however, will not help the child when it needs it, and this prevents the child from 'having the courage' to develop its ego in a normal way; instead the child develops feelings of mistrust, and may become psychotic.

When the child, for some reason or other, has not had the chance to experience early life (up to three years) with one or more loving people, it seems that the internal image of a mother has been spoiled. The Great Mother has manifested herself almost constantly as 'The Evil Mother,' symbolizing chaos, death, drought and hunger. It is thus important to the child to 'return' on a symbolic level to the positive mother-images, to repair it on a symbolic level. A child having experienced early deprivation will somehow be aware of its mother having let it down, but our society and culture tend to try to give the child a romantic idea that the mother is always 'The Great Good Mother'. Consequently, it is easy to understand how many children have feelings of guilt when their mothers have let them down.

If fairy tales are used in a holding environment, they may help the child to gain the understanding that a mother may have both positive and negative traits, also that a person who is not the real (biological) mother could be 'The Good Mother' to the child, helping it to solve problems and gradually becoming responsible and independent. The fairy tales talk to the unconscious on a symbolic level, but they also show practical ways of solving problems, appealing to action, and they give courage and self-confidence.

By starting with a fairy tale in which the child shows interest, one will have a good chance to see the most urgent problems, which the child itself puts in focus. The next thing to do will be to choose a fairy tale which is useful when working with the child's problems. If the main problem is the relationship with the mother, one will choose a fairy tale in which the role of the mother and the symbols attached to her are essential. In this way the fairy tale is a starting point from which the negative mother-image may gradually be changed.

The Favourite Fairy Tale and Guidance Through Fairy Tales
A small boy, Jeff, had been taken away from his mother, as she had threatened to harm him. He was a very greedy and impulse-ridden small boy, who had great difficulty in controlling his emotions, showing much anxiety, particularly when he was going to sleep in the evening. His favourite fairy tale was *Snow White*, which he would want to hear repeatedly. Important to Jeff was the parallel between the rejection of Snow White by the wicked stepmother and his mother's rejection of him, since he had been taken away because she had threatened to harm him. The stepmother also tried to harm Snow White; she tried to kill her. On the conscious level, Jeff did not remember or know anything about his mother which he could talk about, and the episodes which had resulted in him being taken away from home. On the unconscious level, he probably had the same feeling as Snow White. The evil mother has sent him away, thrown him out and threatened to take his life. There were many similarities between the fate of this small boy and that of Snow White.

The fairy tale ends with the evil stepmother being punished; justice has been done. Snow White lives happily to the end of her days. The boy had the chance to feel the pleasure of revenge in a way which did not cause him anxiety. His feelings did not become dangerous. He was obviously pleased when he realized that the wicked mother had been punished, and he was not forced to acknowledge that there was any connection with his own story. He would be neither old nor mature enough to realize this.

The story also illustrates that one can learn to control one's reactions so that they do not disturb positive relationships with other people. The message given to the boy on a conscious level (also on an unconscious level) is that he should learn to postpone the satisfaction of some of his needs and give up something; say no thank you (in the fairy tale it is the beautiful ribbons and the comb, which are given up) in order to grow, to get the kingdom and live happily ever after. Jeff listened to this story several times. Gradually, he became less fascinated by it, and gradually he reached a better understanding of his situation in life.

When this had happened, the boy seemed ready to listen to another fairy tale which could introduce new and positive possibilities. The story could be characterized by the communication of a more positive mother image such as the fairy tale by the brothers Grimm *The Devil with the Three Golden Hairs*. This story is about a boy who is born in a poor home, but with a caul. This is a good omen, and it is told that he shall marry a princess in the future. The king becomes aware of this and to prevent it, he persuades the parents to give away the child. On his way through life the boy meets the good millers, who treat him as their own son and bring him up with care and love.

Later, he seeks shelter in a robber's cave, and here the old woman at the fire takes care of him. When he gets to the castle, the queen welcomes him. Later, he goes to fetch the devil's three golden hairs; it is then the devil's great grand-mother who takes care of him and helps him. All these females symbolize the good mother, and on the unconscious level they may help him to regain the archetypal image of the good mother.

Another choice of fairy tale could be the story of *Pinocchio*. (In the chapter concerning *Pinocchio* as a helper in psychotherapy, there is a description of this story, which illustrates a boy's development from childhood to adulthood.) Although the Good Mother is guiding Pinocchio, as illustrated through the fairy, she does punish him when he is naughty (she pulls his nose, when he is telling lies), but she is also the forgiving mother, who patiently offers him new chances. This story also illustrates the formation of the superego. It is represented by a cricket, which tries to give Pinocchio an understanding of what is right and wrong, something that can help and support him in his further development. In *Pinocchio* one meets the archetypal image of 'The Good Father' in Gepetto. This father image could be important for the boy, since he had not had the experience of a very stable father figure in his first three years of life, and he had reached an age at which it is very important for a boy to turn towards his father and identify with him. Of course, the boy cannot live with a fairy tale father as the only father figure to identify with, but the good father images can help him in the identification process. Since *Pinocchio* is a dramatic story, it might be necessary for the story-teller to make some alterations, adapting it to the child.

In the period when this boy was listening to fairy tales and had the chance to talk about his experiences with the story, he began to grow emotionally and, as I saw it, this had to do with the fairy tale work. It was as if he started to think in a new way, and there was a change in his relationship with his foster parents. It was as if fairy tale reading gave space for a new creative and intuitive way of tackling his problems.

This was a help not only to the boy, but also to his foster parents. It was as if they had got a tool which, on the emotional level, was better to use than the language they normally used when talking with the boy. Various aspects of the fairy tale seemed to fascinate him in different periods. An essential theme concerned mother/stepmother. What does it mean to be a stepmother, and what is a real mother in the biological sense? For a period the boy would play that he was an unborn baby by crawling under the blouse of his foster-mother and being 'born' again, coming out as a baby. He insisted on being attached to her with a ribbon, when they were shopping, since he was afraid of being lost; at least, that was what he said. The play makes one think of the umbilical cord, and it was as if he was trying to 'repair' the disturbed mother-child relationship.

It was obvious that gradually he became more confident with his new home. After quite a long period with these games, he stopped them. This happened at a time when he would say to his foster-mother 'Now you are my real mother, even if you have not given birth to me. This is possible just as a father is also a real father, even if he has not given birth to his child.' While the boy came out with these statements, he was fully aware of the name of his biological mother, and the names of his sisters and brothers. He knew where they lived, and occasionally he was able to talk about them. Jeff seemed to be expressing the feeling that he had accepted his foster-mother as his psychological mother, and on an unconscious level he was repairing the disturbed 'mother image', while being fully aware of his biological background. He also started to make his own fairy tales. One day he told a story about a small kitten. A cat mother and father did not want to have the kitten, even though they were not dying (in fairy tales the hero or heroine often lose their mother because she dies). The kitten was very unhappy, but decided to go out into the world. After some time, it met two big horses, which would very much like to be father and mother, and they took the small kitten, and they all lived happily to the end of their days.

The story had a happy ending, like most fairy tales. By doing something, getting out into the world, the kitten had found what it was longing for, the lost parents. It is a positive story, which seems to illustrate that the boy has a feeling of being able to influence his situation. He has confidence in his own abilities. Of course, horses are odd parents for a kitten; they are not at all like a cat, but they are good enough even so.

During the period in which the kitten tale was made up, Jeff started to remember traumatic events which happened before people took him away from his home. There had been violent episodes, and apparently nobody had ever talked about them with him, and nobody thought he would remember them. One evening, when he had come to bed he said: 'Do you remember the time when you always tied me to the bed?' This question opened up a long talk about what had happened in his life. It had all happened long ago and far away. The distance in time and place was something he was familiar with through fairy tales, and thus it seemed less dangerous and anxiety-provoking to talk about it. Simultaneously, it was possible to support his sense of reality, making him understand that the frightful things really had happened, when he was a very small boy.

Jeff expressed feelings of relief at having reality confirmed, and he said: 'It is so nasty when there is something that you don't know whether is a dream or real.' Having had this talk he stopped screaming and crying when he was put to bed and an earlier habit, where he would always tie himself to something or someone, gradually disappeared.

The fairy tale reading, the conversations following the stories, and Jeff making his own stories, helped him to get into contact with repressed material which had been very conflicting. Having realized through others' confirmation that very nasty things had taken place, that his 'pictures of reality' were right, that it is possible to separate reality from dream, to search for reality and find it, he regained confidence in himself and in others. His behaviour changed in the sense that he became much better at controlling himself in what seemed a healthy way.

Fairy tales can be a gentle and non anxiety-provoking way of bringing earlier conflict material to a level at which one can start to work with it. Another example, illustrating guidance through fairy tales, is about the girl Anja.

Anja was nine years old when her biological mother died. At that age she had only lived for two years with her biological mother. She had lived in nine different foster-families and, as well as this, in different institutions. Anja had been through repeated situations in which she was let down. Her mother left her for the first time when she was three days old. People had threatened her, and she had been a victim of violence and great emotional pressure. She had been completely neglected by her mother, which was not the case with her older sister. The mother was closely attached to Anja's older sister. Anja's ability to tolerate frustration was small, and when she was under stress, she reacted with regression, nervous movements and refused to eat.

Anja had two favourite fairy tales, *Briar Rose* and *Cinderella*. The two fairy tales provided a good opportunity to understand how Anja experienced her situation. *Cinderella* has to do with sibling rivalry and, from a psychodynamic point of view, with a positive working through of the child's developmental crises. The fairy tale would show the parallel to her own mother, who did not protect her from her sister's violent attacks, who preferred the sister and would attack Anja, just as it happens in the fairy tale.

In the fairy tale the sisters and also the stepmother are punished. On the symbolic level, Anja has her revenge without it becoming dangerous to her. But the fairy tale also brings another more positive message. Even if you have to work through many trials during your development, there are good chances of a happy ending, if you are working for it yourself and taking initiatives (the fairy tale illustrates this through Cinderella planting a twig and three times going to the ball).

When looking upon the significance of the fairy tale *Briar Rose,* one will have to take the child's age and developmental level into consideration. Anja had not yet reached puberty. To her, the meeting between the prince and Briar Rose could be understood as the symbol of harmony with oneself and others, and the feeling of a strong ego, a promise that inner chaos could be replaced by harmony. The fairy tale also tells us that this harmony can only occur when it is based on a long period of rest, during which a mature personality can grow. Anja's choice of this fairy tale seems to show that on the unconscious level she is aware of her need for calm and continuity in life so as to develop her ego, and this is probably one reason why this fairy tale appealed to her.

It seemed the fairy tale told Anja and her new family that it is necessary to be patient, have room and time to develop. It seemed important not to force her development. She would need to 'sleep' emotionally, and thus it was no good to comfort her with emotional demands. Like Briar Rose, she had to be 'put to bed' for a long time first. If you impose yourself on her too early, you will not get near her; instead you will get caught on the hawthorn like the early suitors. Not until she has had a rest, been back to a very early and safe position for 'a hundred years', will she be able to express feelings, and the prince will then be able to 'wake' her with his kiss.

From Childhood to Adulthood: Creating Your Own Story

In this book we have written about fairy tale therapy and guidance through fairy tales. We have also tried to illustrate ways in which fairy tale writing could be helpful to the adult person, as was true of the author of *Little Black Sambo*. I have chosen to finish this chapter with a fairy tale written by Mary, a girl of thirteen, who is going through what we would call normal puberty developmental crises, gradually becoming independent from her parents and gradually gaining a new feminine sexual identity. Her fairy tale is one of her ways to work with her personal development. We get the feeling that it has been good for her to write the story. On the unconscious level it seems to have given her the chance to work through thoughts and feelings which were important to her at exactly the period during which she was writing the story.

The Fairy Tale Wood

This story is about five siblings. The two eldest and the youngest are girls and in between there are twin boys. The children go to visit 'the Woman' an old neighbour of ninety-nine years. She tells the children about the dangerous wood 'the fairy tale wood', which she stepped into, when she was young, but seeing a white lady with wicked eyes, she got so frightened that she quickly left it. The wood has been bewitched by a white lady. In the wood there is a treasure containing a claw from a lizard, a tooth from an angry sea-gull, a breath from a tree, and a string from life. If you manage to find these elements and mix them, you will get something wonderful.

The children go into the wood to try their luck. In the wood it feels uncomfortable. You don't hear any sounds from nature, see no animals, you don't feel the wind, and even if there is light in the wood, sun and rain do not get through the canopy. In here the children meet the evil witch, who is ruling over the woods and who has forbidden life to sprout and intends to kill the children.

The children find the witch's castle, where the smallest child gets caught by the witch, while the other children find the treasure. They mix the four elements, and they get hold of a golden key by means of which they set free the animals, life and little Gerda. When the prisoners have been released the key is changed into a diamond. The witch tries to regain her power, but the children cry 'you are not going to give orders, but now we order the rain to come'. The rain is coming, destroying the witch. The wood becomes full of life and happiness and the whistling children return home.

Interpretation

The girl tells her fairy tale as fairy tales are usually told starting 'Once upon a time,' so she creates a distance in relation to time and place. The same distance characterizes her way of talking about the four oldest children, since they have not got real names, and 'the Woman' has not got a name either. All this makes it fairy-tale-like. It is all far away and not very exact or precise. Only the youngest and most innocent of the children has got a 'real' name, 'Gerda'. This seems to help the young author to deal with puberty problems without being too personally involved. Obviously, the fairy tale deals with the development of a girl breaking away, and the attempt to try to find oneself as an independent person. There are small signs suggesting the beginnings of adult sexuality, but the prince is not yet there, and so this is not the central theme. The fairy tale has a happy ending like most fairy tales, and on a symbolic level it thus seems to promise a positive solution of the puberty-crisis.

The fairy tale starts with the woman having lived her life. She passes it on to the children through her memory about 'the dangerous wood', which might have to do with memories concerning youth. Puberty with beginning adult sexuality, fight for independence from parental influence, opposition and searching for personal identity, which 'the woman' remembers, but may not have ventured to live through, telling that she fled from the wood and home to safety. In the fairy tale she has not become a complete person with her own name or individuality, she is 'the woman'. As for the children, we hear that they had never been in the wood before; but there has to be a first time, and so they went into the wood, into a new period of life, into the unknown, into puberty. In the wood they will try to find the treasure consisting of (1) a string from life, (2) a breath from a tree, (3) a tooth from an angry sea gull and (4) a claw from a lizard.

Looking at the treasure, a string from life, it is natural to think of the umbilical cord and the close connection with the mother, the untouched nature, the unspoiled small child. It seems possible to become angry, get into opposition, become free – flying away without it being dangerous. An angry sea-gull is not a very dangerous bird. A lizard from the past could show that you will always carry the past with you into the future. A breath from a tree seems to indicate life and good feelings. If you mix these four things, you get something 'absolutely wonderful'. The treasure seems to promise that the girl is able to get free through puberty, with its anger – 'fly away from the nest', find herself as a complete person. She will still be able to integrate the positive traits from the innocent child, the positive relationship with her mother when reaching her final adult identity.

The children now agree upon trying their luck. 'They had never been in the wood before. The mother made a picnic-lunch for them to take with. She knew that the children would go out into the wood, but she thought they would merely play.' The children enter life and puberty on their own, but the mother, symbolized through what Neumann (1976) calls the archetypal image of 'The Good Mother' makes sure that it is possible by providing them with a picnic lunch. They have the basic trust, which is necessary to development.

The mother knew that they would go out into the wood, but she thought they would merely play. The mother has seen to it that the children have the chance to develop independence and adulthood, but she has not yet realized very clearly that they are on their way. She still sees them as children. We meet the same picture when the witch is catching the smallest child, locking it up. This could be interpreted as the mother's attempt to hold on to the girl, seeing her as the small dependent child needing to be guided by her mother. We see the mother's resistance to letting the child grow up, and thus the negative aspects of the mother-figure.

'They walked and walked and after an hour, they came to the fairy tale wood.' This is a message about action. The children do something and have to do something so as to continue their development. Having got into the wood the children sit down and eat their lunch, the symbol of the connection with past times and with the mother. However, at the place where they sit down to eat, the sun cannot pass through to them. As for the symbolic significance of the sun, one might suggest that the god of the sun was Apollo a masculine symbol.

According to Neumann, the sun is the symbol of the father, and in this story, there is no connection with the masculine aspects (animus). The sun also symbolizes the power to gain greater understanding of oneself.

What we are dealing with seems to be a period during which the ego is going to get free from female power and enter developmental stages which require more masculine strength. This happens through a rebellion against the mother and, to legitimize this, the mother must be 'the Evil Mother' for some time. Finally, the archetypal picture of 'The Great Mother' should be there, combining the positive and negative.

As for Mary, we also get the feeling that she is opposing her father. She needs the creative, masculine powers to develop her own personality, but the father is too far away emotionally, since the sun will not get through to her. In this way we also sense the opposition to her father on an unconscious level.

In the fairy tale it happens that the children experience the good, nurturing caring mother. Then they meet the 'Evil Mother' symbolizing death and destruction, as illustrated through the witch, who gets destroyed. The child has been fighting and it has won the power struggle. 'You are not going to give orders,' cried the children, and now they can return home whistling. They have gone further in their development and can return to their mother. The mother now has less influence, her position is not as central, and the children are more free.

The same things are illustrated in the scene where the treasure gets mixed and changed into a golden key, which again is changed into a diamond. So 'the animals, life and little Gerda' get free. On the symbolic level gold shows increased self-awareness and psychological values concerning the eternal, the non-transitory, which cannot be destroyed by earthly forces. For precious stones, the symbolic significance is the same, but to a much greater extent. The diamond is hard/solid in its form and cannot easily be changed. The child, the young one, has found itself its 'final' identity, which cannot be changed from now on, but can be polished to become richly faceted.

In the story it says: 'Neither could they hear Nature's own sounds, and not one animal could be seen. No wind could be felt and neither sun nor rain could come through to the canopies.' The children cannot see, nor hear, nor feel and nothing gets through to them, which could be seen as the illustration of strong egocentricity often characterizing puberty; a standstill, an introversion concentrating on personal needs 'walking into the wood,' into oneself, a preoccupation with oneself, introversion. Simultaneously, you find a certain distance to other peoples' emotions and needs. A period in which it is necessary for the young ones to be preoccupied with themselves, excluding the earlier 'creator of norms', particularly the parents, so they might peacefully find themselves in an independent and individual personality.

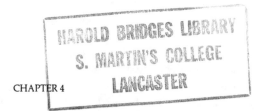
CHAPTER 4

Fairy Tale Conversations

Ernst W. Pedersen

Chaplaincy in a Psychiatric Hospital

Defining a hospital chaplain's role is no easy matter. Traditionally, his primary duties and tasks have been to celebrate services, tell the stories that make up the bible, administer the nurturing sacraments and attend to the personal religious needs of the patients. Within these limited current pastoral care services, the hospital chaplain has had his competence.

In a psychiatric hospital, he does, in addition, a great deal of pastoral counselling. He engages the patients in religious education, delivers lectures on religious and cultural topics, and, as in my own case, employs the use of fairy tale conversations. That does not mean that the chaplain necessarily becomes part of the mental health team, but, through his knowledge of psychology and deeper psychological theories applied to fairy tale interpretations, in addition to his theological knowledge, he may be able to offer a complementary approach to alleviating the multifaceted sufferings of mentally disturbed people. He may thus contribute to making their conditions a bit less chaotic, more under-standable, and thus meaningful for them.

When arranging fairy tale conversations with psychiatric patients, it is important for all the participating staff members to try to understand the patients' symbolic world. And the staff members should be aware of signals from the participating patients to see if there is a need for follow-up contacts between meetings. A spiritual reflection on life will often make the patients' otherwise dull existence in the wards more stimulating and rewarding. In a holistic model of communication, such as the one constituted by fairy tale conversation groups, there is no limit to the topics that a patient may address. The patient's entire being may be focused on in this form of group guidance.

Through this approach, the hospital chaplain can become a resource person (in a broader sense) who may serve both patients and staff members in facing their common and individual problems. After all, the patients are not very different from the rest of us. There is no reason to sentimentalize them and describe them as helpless victims of injurious internal or external processes nor to induce in them a false sense of the authority of their sane fellows. Rather, the purpose is to have them join a conversational relationship in which all those present are of equal value. Such acceptance of the patients can promote in them at least a momentary wellbeing, as is testified by staff members. This, in turn, can increase their self confidence and release their blocked potential to change and grow.

Through fairy tale conversations, many difficult individual problems can be simplified or turned into problems which everyone shares. In other words, private symbols, i.e. noncommunicative substitutional symbols for traumata beyond endurance, may be converted to communicable public symbols. In this form they may be obtainable for a conversational adaption to the circumstances of outer reality, and made comprehensible through the symbolic, but lucid experiences of the fairy tale characters. This will diminish their apprehensive effect.

The symbolic 'salvation' from one's past may have a momentary relieving, comforting and supporting influence on the personal condition of the patients when they are listening to or participating in fairy tale interpretations, even if their mental illness is chronic and not likely to be decisively changed. Furthermore, these fairy tale group gatherings express an attitude of acceptance and respect for the individual patient as a person, who belongs to a community in which all the members have a common field of experience regarding human areas of conflict. This, of course, includes a more or less viable religious perspective on the patient's life.

In presenting to the patients their own human condition as it is described in the fairy tales, the narrator and the attending staff members can provide an emotional presence in which healing of the ill may occur, although not necessarily a curing of the illness. Such a feeling of coherence may be a key resource for the patients in their attempt to cope with the living conditions of chronic mental illness or may help them to come to terms with a limited period in a psychiatric hospital.

If care providers are to enable people in crisis to find meaning through fairy tales, they must be ready to enter the painful world of those who are suffering, as symbolized by the circumstances of the fairy tales told. By interpreting the symbols indirectly, they must show an empathic understanding of the world of the participants in the conversation. The story-teller must be willing to engage in the struggle and emphasise with the vulnerability by which mentally ill persons are engulfed. In order to be able to accomplish this, the imaginative narrator must be at home with his or her own inner world. Fairy tale interpretation and conversation may be a way of sharing failure and grief with a person at critical times of his life and a means of restoring a valuable resource for mental recovery.

Patient in a Psychiatric Hospital

The period of a person's life spent in a psychiatric hospital may provide as great a chance for personality development, maturity growth and increase of personal insight as the time spent outside the hospital walls. Perhaps even a greater chance, if the necessary resources of psychotherapy and pastoral counselling in a cooperating combination of the two are available.

In times of struggling with decreasing funding, there is a reduced availability of psychotherapeutic intervention. The same may hold true for the availability of pastoral care. Even so, it is a very important condition for an optimal ancillary service for people with psychological disturbances, that chaplains be able to combine pastoral care with an extensive psychotherapeutic understanding of the psychopathological mechanisms involved.

Actually, a significant number of delusions and distorted ideas have been derived from religious sources. When the chaplain appears among the patients, he is often bombarded with questions about religious matters. Whether based on a correct or on a delusional understanding of religious matters, these questions, on closer inspection, usually turn out to be common philosophical, psychological and religious questions which reflect the questioner's own personal problems.

In a certain sense, the biography of our individual histories or our personal developments, as well as that of mankind, has been recorded in myths, in the Holy Scriptures of the great world religions and in fairy tales. It is therefore not surprising that, when religion is part of a patient's psychosocial history, inquiry into the meaning of life and other fundamental existential questions is repeatedly focused on in periods of personal crisis. In dealing with these problems it is a prerequisite that all participants in the fairy tale conversation are willing to try to understand the 'symbol language' – 'the only foreign language everyone should know', according to Fromm (1951).

It is easy for admission to a hospital as mentally ill to cause a feeling of being pushed away from normal and sane human relations. The surroundings are, of course, different, but usually that will be accepted during the necessary period of hospitalization. It may be more difficult to come to terms with abnormal behaviour in the community of fellow-patients.

A mental illness may in itself dispose one to a feeling of loneliness, often with paranoid features causing a state of insecurity. The patient's feeling of being isolated in the ward diminishes through his participation in a fairy tale conversation about normal or traumatic human conditions, as they are reflected in the narrative of the fairy tale. The way the fairy tale characters manage human conflicts serves as a model for coping with everyday life. Being thus confronted with the experiences of the normal life in which they have failed, participants are now offered a safer position from which they may view their conflicts and thus another way in which to form new and better patterns for life after their discharge.

In the fairy tale conversation process itself, confidence is increased by the fact that no treatment is being carried out; no result has to be achieved. Whatever the participants receive, there are no strings attached. Psychological manipulation is avoided; no psychotherapeutic or preaching efforts take place. By regarding a mental illness as a response to discouraging conditions, there *might* be a therapeutic effect if the individual patient becomes aware of *his or her own* (more or less limited) possibilities of trying to alter his response to the questions arising from his mental disturbance or from the symbols of his delusions.

The fairy tale interpretation aims at a holistic view of human existence; it does not try to concentrate on a single symptom or problem. If it is conducted in a spirit of friendship, and acceptance of the patient, the illness may temporarily 'be forgotten' – 'vanish' in the greater context. The patient will then no longer feel victimized or experience himself as an object of somebody's care, but rather as a person who himself co-operates and contributes to the caring process. Care is essentially mutual, and in realizing this, the patient may dimly cherish a hope of being able to bring about transformations in his present condition; transformations towards greater wholeness and harmony.

It is up to the individual person whether or not he or she will enter into his or her own history (myth, tale) and follow the paths of wisdom shown in them. The will to do so is essential and ultimately one's own responsibility. 'Will you recover?' Jesus asked the lame man whom he cured. To the extent that disease may be seen behaviourally as a person's response to a conflict, that person will have to answer the question: 'Will you solve your conflict?' If he replies in the affirmative, he may 'live happily ever after' – as some fairy tales put it – even in the face of adversities. It depends on a decision which may be facilitated significantly by carefully planned and well executed assistance.

The Narrative Way

In the title *Fairy Tale Conversations* of this chapter, the word 'conversation', meaning associating and talking with, is quite an accurate description of the method. The participants are talking together on the basis of the events that occur in the particular fairy tale chosen for the group.

At the first meeting the text is read out *in extenso*; this is frequently done by one of the patients in the group. Then the hospital chaplain provides an introduction to the fairy tale and a narrative interpretation of the first part of it. This interpretation continues at the following meetings, and it is offered to the patients with an invitation to reinterpret and modify. As the possibilities of expounding are limited only by the imagination of the group-members, it may take 10 to 12 one-hour meetings to interpret one fairy tale in some detail.

Answers to questions are sought in a dialogue rather than being readily dispensed. This is true to the nature of the matter, because symbols are ambiguous and multidimensional. At the same time, they are clear and illustrative, and are therefore excellent substitutional expressions for conflicting matters which do not transform into abstract ideas. In spite of their fantastic forms, fairy tales contain a human realism that enables the patients to deal constructively with the inner forces (which guide their behaviour) at a symbolic distance.

This kind of group dialogues provides a sort of non-authoritarian inter-personal relationship without any means of coercion. Authority emerges of itself whenever something right and essential is told or done. A dialogue such as this is an exchange of thoughts in which the amplification of the fairy tale matter, and the associative communication deriving from it, puts the participants in touch with each other's unconscious in an intentional holistic perspective. A free conversation in accord with the unconscious of the participants will gener-ally emerge as a very agreeable undertaking. Such a conversation is not treat-ment, but it is assumed to have a therapeutic effect not unlike the curative effect of love, which is not considered treatment either. It seems to be a gentle way in which to establish contact with one's inner images, because the participants are allowed to avoid the suppressed conflicts portrayed and stay with the characters of the fairy tale. To know that brings about a soothing feeling of comfort.

The Conversation Material

In the old days, the story-teller came into a village to tell the traditional stories at an hour when the rhythm of the day was setting a mood for listening. These tales would help settle the unconscious inner conflicts of the village-people. In a similar way, the hospital chaplain comes to the ward at an appropriate time and sits down among the patients, who have been invited to the group, in order to tell them a traditional story in which they may find anew their own individual story – the story, which perhaps cannot be remembered coherently because of suppression of the greater part of it. In so doing, he may strengthen the listeners' perception of patterns of their lives, thus making these patterns conscious and evident to the participants.

For this purpose, the fairy tales are advantageous because of their feeling for the value of concrete objects. Things remain more real than mental states; they are therefore more suitable and lucid as symbols serving as psychic energy-transformers (Hark 1988, p.157). Thus objects may refer to a wisdom that provides release.

> 'Told by generation after generation, the traditional stories projected the deepest wishes of the folk, generalized diverse characters into a few types, selected the incidents that would most strikingly illustrate what heroes and heroines, witches, enchanters, giants and dwarfs, the haughty, the envious and the unfaithful were capable of' (Grimm 1972, p.xi).

Fairy tales are representative of the archetypical powers within each person. At the same time they contain a belief in the victory of the good forces. The positive intentions predominate, and that is essential for sustaining hope during a stay in hospital. These prevailing intentions provide hope of solving the conflicts of the past as well as of the present in the best possible way.

For this purpose, the fairy tales collected by the Brothers Grimm (1972) are unsurpassed. These tales offer a world which can easily be interpreted as symbolic of actual life. The narrator amplifies the story with new material derived from inner and outer sources which represent common conditions that are comparable with the participants in a group conversation.

Examples of Subjects for Fairy Tale Conversations

Regarding the choice of the fairy tales for group conversations, my endeavour is to find general human motives which may inspire most people's capability for association. Considering first a group of young patients, it is relevant to choose fairy tales dealing with the psychological conditions for the development of maturity.

In *Hänsel and Gretel* (Brudal 1984, pp.102–105) there is a symbolic description of the frustration and rejection that every child has in some way experienced during the first seven years of life. 'The two children also had not been able to sleep for hunger.' Hunger symbolizes deprivation. 'We will take the children out into the forest to where it is the thickest.' The forest here symbolizes the loss of values and safety. They try to find their way back (i.e. regression) but there is no other way out than forward (i.e. development). 'Gretel wept bitter tears and said to Hänsel: "Now all is over with us." "Be quiet, Gretel," said Hänsel, "do not distress yourself, I will soon find a way to help us."' As shown in these lines, Gretel represents the emotional life and Hänsel the cognitive efforts to survive the crisis of separation. And at last the conflict is solved: they can return to their home, emotionally and intellectually enriched, as symbolized by pearls and jewels. Through the misery, they gain new values for their future lives.

The next step in life is symbolically illustrated by the fairy tale about Little Snow-White (Brudal 1984, pp.106–109) and covers the years from seven to fourteen. In those years preceding puberty, the child has to overcome the hurdle of 'passing from self-interest to self-interestedness' (Allport 1967, p.35). The child may find that extremely difficult. 'But now the poor child was alone in the great forest, and so terrified that she looked at all the leaves on the trees, and did not know what to do'. The seven years in the forest is a time in which the child encounters grave disappointments and deprivation.

With her maturing intelligence, which by now is able to comprehend somewhat more adequately, she learns to be responsible for herself. 'She ran as long as her feet would go until it was almost evening; then she saw a little cottage and went into it to rest herself.' And here she came to know her 'seven dwarfs, who dug and delved in the mountain for ore'. They are characters symbolic of more instinctive aspects of human life and very useful. They are gone during the day-time, but appear in our dream-life at night, being instrumental in the solution of both practical everyday problems and the deep-rooted problems of life. Here the participants are brought into contact with the spiritual values of the mind, while the envious queen, the stepmother, represents the preoccupation with material, superficial things. She 'could not bear that anyone else should surpass her in beauty'.

In the conversational interpretation, this may refer to the developing sentiment for internalized religious objects as the child gradually begins to approximate her theology to more mature forms and dissociates herself from the projective conceptions. At last, the wicked queen 'dropped down dead', indicating the survival of the true and eternal values of life as symbolized by the celebration of Snow White's wedding 'with great show and splendour'.

This sequence of fairy tales may be concluded with *The Little Briar-Rose* (Brudal 1984, pp.109–111) which represents the adolescence period between fourteen and twenty-one. During this period, the youth is compelled to transform most of his attitudes. Often there is a period of rebellion, although in some cases the transition is fluent and imperceptible. So it seems to be for Little Briar-Rose, even if the beginning of the story is dramatic.

After the birth of the girl, a 'feast was held with all manner of splendour, and the [twelve] Wise Women bestowed their magic gifts upon the baby' but the thirteenth 'wished to avenge herself for not having been invited', and so 'she cried with a loud voice: "The King's daughter shall in her fifteenth year prick herself with a spindle, and fall down dead."'

The deep sleep, however, in which she lies, is a symbolic expression for an integrative connection between the conscious and the unconscious. The child in itself, being a picture of renewal, development and growth, shall be whole. Her sleep is a symbolic death and rebirth to a new life.

This provides the opportunity to touch on the suicidal syndrome as well as the problems of preventing suicide. The story opens up a deeper understanding of the fact that it is not the body that should be killed; rather it is something in the inner world that has to be changed ('killed') as a condition or basis for the 'resurrection' of new and healed spiritual life. Suicide is not an entrance to a fanciful new life, but a killing of the body, which prevents a change to a new life as opposed to the spiritual renewal which may provoke really new and creative possibilities for a meaningful life. Talking about this widespread phenomenon of our time may be extremely helpful for patients considering suicide.

In itself, the sleep of the girl symbolizes her slow growing up to an integrated and harmonic psychic whole, which awakens when she is united with her hero (i.e. her cognitive side is united with her emotional side). This corresponds to what happens in the suicide-prevention work. 'But as soon as he kissed her, Briar-Rose opened her eyes and awoke, and looked at him sweetly... And then the marriage was celebrated with all splendour, and they lived contented to the end of their days.'

However, before reaching that contended state of the union of opposites (*conjunctio oppositorum*), a long developmental process may have to be negotiated, as indicated by the words of the fairy tale: 'But by this time the hundred years had just passed, and the day had come when Briar-Rose was to awake again' – a hundred years being a symbolic expression for a long time.

In continuation of the psycho-developmental perspective of the three preceding fairy tales, *The Cat with the Boots* (Kaufmann 1985) may also be selected. This is an outstanding symbolic description of a young man's path to becoming master or King in his own internal kingdom. Being the youngest son of three, the boy in the story inherited only a cat when his father, the miller, died. But what a cat! He soon became aware that this cat was his internal guide. All he had to do was to give it a pair of boots. This is a symbolic expression of his personality maturing. The cat showed him what he could and should be, and acted as his helpful servant and guide through his entire life.

Interpreting the particular events of the young man's life story in a conversational way, among other things, help patients who have not finished old grief to do so. 'But the miller died, and his sons divided his properties left between them.' And he who got the cat 'fetched a deep sigh'. This is a situation most people have experienced, so it provides the opportunity to talk about loss and grief and how to resolve, reformulate and transform loss (Schneider 1984, pp.72–74). Depending on how far the individual participant in the conversation is ready to go, this may involve tracing back the processes related to loss and the discovery of unresolved patterns of grief.

The young man's bathing in the river – when the cat arranged for his clothes to be changed with those, new and fashionable, of a count – may serve as another example of a conversation subject. The bathing may be seen as a symbol of baptism, of renewal and finding a new way in life through the help of the cat, his internal adviser. Obviously, religious aspects may be dealt with too.

The entire fairy tale *The Cat with the Boots*, is a marvellous, varied representation of the mutual touch of the instinctive, the animalistic and the human aspects of the developing personality, resulting in a wholeness of mind. In telling and talking about such aspects, somebody may come to be aware of unsettled conflicts influencing the present but stemming from childhood and the turbulent years of adolescence. And through his improved understanding of the circumstances involved and of mental processes, he may gain insight into a new and better way to manage these.

Other fairy tales focus on the developmental issues of couple crisis. *The Fisherman and His Wife* (Kast 1983, pp.20–35) represents this kind of experience. We meet a couple with very different views on new approaches and changes in the matrimonial life. The fisherman was very easy to satisfy and seemingly contented with a stationary way of life. 'He was sitting with his rod, looking at the clear water, and he sat and he sat'. His wife, on the other hand, was a more dynamic person. '"Husband," said the woman, "have you caught nothing

to-day?" "No," said the man, "I did catch a Flounder, who said he was an enchanted prince, so I let him go again." "Did you not wish for anything first?" said the woman. "No," said the man; "what should I wish for?"' *His* imagination was too limited, so *her* wishes became increasingly exaggerated. He was a dormant partner who let everything remain as it was, and she knew no limits to her greed. Consequently, their conflict escalated, and 'the sea...was no longer so smooth'. Their wills were in conflict: the man was an obsessive character and the woman a rather hysterical personality. As the fisherman himself put it:

> 'For my wife, good Ilsabil,
> Wills not as I'd have her will.'

It requires great skill to join together such extremes. First of all, the fisherman must realize that even if it be Ilsabil who expresses all the desires, he himself is covetous of the very same things; only he does not have the courage to admit it. He certainly agrees with her saying '...it is surely hard to have to live always in this pig-sty'. The pig-sty is a symbol of the very narrow limits within which they are living in every respect, spiritually as well as materially. If they reach an understanding of their differing personality features, they may obtain a better communication about their shared desires. This would make her cravings, more moderate and his more daring.

The Flounder is a symbol of the potentials they actually have in common; all they have to do is to learn to use them appropriately. But they do not. The opposites are not counterbalanced: the fisherman represents the resignation (he has given up to wish), while his wife desires what 'is impossible to man's power' (*Matthew* 19:26). Therefore, they are thrown back to disastrous conditions, in that they find themselves 'back again in the pig-sty' having lived in a palatial habitation. As a somewhat rare exception, this fairy tale has an unhappy ending, indicating that in life this is also a very real contingency. Hubris will forever be punished.

A happy ending of a couple crisis with a basis in early childhood is shown in another relevant fairy tale: *The Frog-King, or Iron-Henry* (Jellouschek 1985, pp.40–45, 109–111). The very first line refers to a happy ending: 'In olden times when wishing still helped one'. So it is right at the beginning asserted that wishing helps; a good starting point for a group conversation. It suggests that the will to wish may be helpful in itself. At first, wishing helped the beautiful daughter of the King when she played with her 'golden ball...by the side of the cool fountain' in the forest and lost it, because 'it happened that on one occasion it did not fall into her little hand, but on to the ground beyond, and rolled straight into the water'.

The golden ball can be seen as a symbol of what is valuable in life. In this case it may be her childhood, her existence as the King, her father's, dearest child, a position that she was losing. When she realized she had lost her ball, she was shocked and 'began to cry, and cried louder and louder' until 'someone said to her: "What ails you, King's daughter?" And she saw a frog stretching forth its big ugly head from the water. "Ah! old watersplasher, is it you?" she said; "I am weeping for my golden ball, which has fallen into the well."' And then the frog promised to 'bring her plaything up again', if she in return would love the frog and allow it to 'be her companion and play-fellow, to sit by her at her table, and eat off her little golden plate, and drink out of her little cup, and sleep in her little bed'. '"Oh, yes," she said, "I promise you all you wish."'

Her expectations were that the frog would bring her back her lost childhood and give her the safety she knew from her father's palace. But, as she understood what her promise obliged her to do, she was even more shocked than when she lost the golden ball. Actually, she had agreed to marry the ugly frog. In the interpretation, the further events in their lives together may be viewed as an exploration of a young couple's development of human and matrimonial potentials.

Complications in trying to overcome the fragmentary, and find wholeness as a couple may be caused by the fact that no mother seems to be present in the palace of the King. The princess had no role model during her years of growth. Likewise, the frog obviously had no father as a role model, but only a witch, who had cast a spell on him, i.e. a mother who, herself lacking in love, has not been able to let go of him. His experience of the female-motherly aspects in life had been a negative one. This common 'inheritance' influenced their partner-ship in such a way that they 'loved' each other because they *needed* each other. Hidden needs, which they will not be able to admit to, emerge repeatedly in their conversation.

Discussing such communication-blocks during the conversations may aid participants with similar troubles to reach a better understanding of these relating processes. This,in turn, may lead to small steps in implementing mutual growth in their couple-relating. Hence, after solving all the troubles, 'they went to sleep, and next morning, when the sun awoke them, a carriage came driving up with eight white horses, and behind stood the young King's servant, the faithful Iron-Henry'. The bewitched frog was delivered from the well by the princess and had become a young King who took his bride with him into his kingdom, because he 'was set free and was happy'.

Thus both of them were free in their love, so they did not any more tell each other 'I love you, because I need you.' but 'I need you, because I love you!' In this fairy tale, possibilities that had not previously occurred to either of the two partners are revealed.

Especially appreciated by the patients are fairy tales dealing with general problems of life. Interpretations of occurrences and incidents in everyday life may have a great impact on the degree of success with which these are en-countered and turned to the best possible account. In that respect, the fairy tale *Hans in Luck* (Zielen 1987, pp.21–24, 142) may be unsurpassed. 'Hans had served his master for seven years, so he said to him: "Master, my time is up; now I should be glad to go home to my mother; give me my wages." And he gave Hans a piece of gold as big as his head.'

Hans had served for seven years. To begin with, the number 'seven' provides material for a comprehensive conversation. According to the myth of creation in *Genesis*, God, at the beginning of time, created heaven and earth in six days and rested on the seventh day, when 'all the furniture of them were completed' and 'his whole task accomplished' (*Genesis* 1–2). Such an amplification is often a good starting point for an extensive religious education. Seven is a symbolic number for wholeness, for something completed. It has from time immemorial been considered a holy number for consummation as well as for a new beginning.

Both of these viewpoints apply to *Hans in Luck*. His 'time is up'. He has finished a period of his life. The 'piece of gold as big as his head' may be a symbol for the accomplishments and the wisdom he has gained from the master during that time. And endowed with these 'wages', he 'set out on his way home'. It looks as if Hans has developed certain emotional and spiritual qualities which make it possible for him to face the world in an unusual way. When he exchanged his gold for a horse, the horse for a cow, the cow for a pig, the pig for a goose, and the goose for a grindstone, he felt himself to 'be the luckiest fellow on earth', because 'he had always made such good bargains'. This view is his own alternative interpretation of what anybody else would call to be taken in. But for Hans, each 'bargain' gives him just what he needs to be cheered up so he can make progress on his way 'home to his mother'. The mother symbolizes the ultimate goal of his life which every exchange provides him with the means to attain.

At this point in the conversation, it is relevant to talk about the price of not being like anybody else, and how important it is to be committed to the changing games of life. This involves testing the true value of things as means of attaining one's end. And even if Hans was 'thrown off' the horse, and 'not a drop of milk' came from the cow, and he was cheated in all the other bargains too, he nevertheless was understood to profit from it by realizing the true values of life. Those values are very often inconsistent with the opinion of the majority of people, which mostly attaches importance to materialistic advantages, to 'pieces of gold', resulting in – as Hans put it – the fact that 'I cannot hold my head straight for it, and it hurts my shoulder'.

Having had conversations about Hans's use of the worldly goods for ten to twelve hours during as many meetings, we have gained a better understanding of the reason why Hans at last 'with a light heart and free from every burden cried out: "There is no man under the sun so fortunate as I."' Hans in Luck was, as matter-of-fact, lucky. In some way, it is as if man needs a proper medley of prosperity and adversity in order to be able to experience what might be called happiness.

This faculty for getting the best out of everything we meet again in the fairy tale *The Valiant Little Tailor* (Müller 1985, pp.25–6; 33–6, 60–6). But the way in which the tailor obtains his success is not quite so simple-minded as the way Hans in Luck went about it. In many respects, the little tailor is quite a cunning person who not only – as Hans in Luck – passively reinterprets all occurrences of unforeseen disadvantageous events for his own sake. His brain is functioning excellently. Instead of physical strength, he uses logic. His slyness and intuition always enable him to figure out how he can be equal to the occasion and get him out of even very dangerous and delicate situations on his way through the world. He is successful in spite of the frail constitution tailors often had.

In a conversational approach to *The Valiant Little Tailor*, this point may offer a good opening theme: the fundamental weakness of man. Life is always greater and stronger than man. If it is explained to the group members what that means, psychologically and religiously, they may be encouraged to be on the lookout for other possibilities of compensation for the absence of some physical or mental power – just as the little tailor compensated for the lack of a strong constitution.

First, we could ask the little tailor to teach us the art of dealing with the powers and energies of life in a sensible way. Thus, we may discover that he can teach us the art of living. What *is* the art of living, after all? We might suggest it to be an attitude towards trying to recognize the wholeness of life; the contrasts as well as the multiplicity and the unceasing changes, and through all that achieve an adequate and continuous joy in life. In short, it is the art of getting the best out of one's life.

The Valiant Little Taylor shows us that the art of living begins with consciousness of the inherent weaknesses of life. Recognizing this truth enables the participants to cooperate with life-energy and not counteract it. As a consequence, it may also be natural to submit to the influence of greater powers. In *The New Testament*, St. Paul expresses this wisdom in his second letter to the Corinthians: 'More than ever, then, I delight to boast of the weaknesses that humiliate me, so that the strength of Christ may enshrine itself in me... When I am weakest, then I am strongest of all' (II *Corinthians* 12:9–10).

Elaborating such different angles of incidence may be profitable in discovering new ways of facing one's own existence. So the conversation may not only fill a vacant hour, but fill it with symbolic fare. 'And since symbolization is the characteristic pleasure of the human mind, the fascination of the tale increases in proportion to the richness of its symbolic content' (Campbell 1972, p.862).

Already the first few words of the fairy tale promulgate a pleasant feeling of zest for life: 'One summer's morning a little tailor was sitting on his table by the window; he was in good spirits, and sewed with all his might'. The fairy tale describes the very beginning a summer morning. In the cycle of nature, and in the phases of man's life, the summertime indicates a period of unfolding of all immanent energies, of growth and of differentiating.

An additional connotation would be to become aware of the summer as a symbol for what can be achieved in every phase of life. Each age has its developmental and maturing tasks. Hence, each age may be seen as 'the peak of life' contrary to the generally accepted view in the industrial society, that only the age during which there is the highest capacity for work has a value, thus leaving childhood and old age – together with limited or lasting periods of somatic or psychic illness – in darkness as having lesser or no worth. Then, the art of living is to realize that each stage of life has its summertime.

As another associative jumping-off board – the window – is very suitable. 'The Little Tailor was sitting…by the window.' So the art of living is also to find out how to get a sunny place at a window. Considering the window as a symbol of the eyes may lead to the realization of the essentials of a good view of all forms and colours of the living world. Sitting at this window, he had the opportunity to buy some 'good jams' from 'a peasant woman', who 'came…down the street crying: "Good jams, cheap!"'

> '[But] the smell of the street jam rose to where the flies were sitting in great numbers, and they were attracted and descended on it in hosts. "Hi! Who invited you?" said the little tailor… The little tailor at last lost all patience, and drew a piece of cloth from the hole under his work-table, and saying: "Wait, and I will give it to you," struck it mercilessly on them. When he drew it away and counted, there lay before him no fewer than seven, dead and with legs stretched out. "Are you a fellow of that sort?" said he, and could not help admiring his own bravery. "The whole town shall know of this!" said he. And the little tailor hastened to cut himself a girdle, stitched it, and embroidered on it in large letters: "Seven at one stroke!"'

Here we meet again the number seven, signifying a completed task. The experience of accomplishing such a deed, although he exaggerates his courage somewhat, alters his future fate decisively. From this experience, he makes himself a 'symbol of power', i.e. his girdle with the imposing words: 'Seven at one stroke!' This appears afterwards to be a powerful symbol that impresses everybody and, last but not least, he himself is encouraged merely by thinking of it. In other words, the little tailor has demonstrated his ability to solve a practical problem. Thus he has increased his self-confidence and, while knowing very well about his weakness, this symbol of power encourages him to tell the world of his strength. '"What, the town!" he continued, "the whole world shall hear of it!" and his heart wagged with joy like a lamb's tail.'

Having mastered all the other trials on his way through life such as defeating 'powerful giants', 'a roaming unicorn' and 'a wild boar', 'the little tailor married the King's daughter' whereupon 'he was and remained a king to the end of his life'. Here 'the King' may symbolize his true inner identity, the real value of the tailor in spite of his littleness. And so he symbolizes everyone who has reached so far in his mature development that he has perceived his own ultimate

_J. Through that, he may avoid, partly a superhuman presumption, partly a life-spoiling defeat. He remains flexible, hence he cannot be broken.

A similar flexible attitude can be observed in *Cinderella* (Wöller 1984, pp.21–3, 47–9, 68–73, 126) although her survival and success depend on goodness, piety and gentleness rather than on the cunning and boasting of the little tailor. *Cinderella*, in a way, takes us back to the mythical past of mankind. Once the earth was the dwelling-place of the Great Mother. Under her protection this world was still a safe home for plants and animals, for sons and daughters, for fruitfulness and vitality; in short, a dwelling-place facilitating a caring and continual renewal of life. But this original matriarchy was succeeded by the domination of the male part of mankind, a patriarchy.

In this era, importance was predominantly attached to physical power and technical skill rather than to womanly values such as care and love. This caused a lot of misery, trouble and war, and had devastating influences on nature. *Homo faber* had banished the female aspects of human existence to the heap of ashes, to a 'Cinderella-existence'. That is, among other things, what the fairy tale *Cinderella* reflects in its quest for the revival of the partly lost view that love is an energy which is able to overcome envy as well as physical and psychic violence.

From this point of view, we will find spiritual treasures in abundance in the troublesome experiences of Cinderella. The sad beginning of her life story goes: 'The wife of a rich man fell sick, and as she felt that her end was drawing near, she called her only daughter to her bedside and said: 'Dear child, be good and pious, and then the good God will always protect you, and I will look down on you from Heaven and be near you.' Even if the beginning is sad, we know – having read the whole tale – that for Cinderella everything turns out well. This may induce in the participants a hope for a happier life in spite of even great losses and troubles. Cinderella has lost her protecting mother, but somehow the mother's spiritual care is still there to guide her through all adversities.

To be good and pious means keeping alive the memory of the female and maternal values she was taught by her mother. And this she has to do under extremely difficult circumstances in the patriarchy which took over with her father's remarriage. His new wife and her two daughters had, all three of them, rejected the true female values and were content with the superficial state of being part of a rich man's front in 'beautiful dresses' and plastered with 'pearls and jewels'. The motherly aspects, such as caring, loving and supporting (to 'carry water, light fires, cook and wash'), are reduced to a despicable occupation; symbolically, they are reduced to 'cinders', hence the name 'Cinderella'.

Due to this feeling of inferiority, many women are prevented from achieving the success and prestige which they deserve in professional life. This 'Cinderella-complex' is a widespread phenomenon, as demonstrated in a book of that title by the American psychologist Colette Dowling. This inferiority complex plays a significant role in many neurotic and depressive states among the psychiatric patients.

Cinderella may refer to problems of relating to the family during the years of puberty, to matrimonial conflicts and a great number of topics concerning material and spiritual poverty or wealth. Although the mother's grave is the decisive symbol of the spiritual power which secures her future happiness, Cinderella obviously also needs her father. He remains in the background, but gave her 'the hazel twig', she had wished for, when he bought 'beautiful dresses, pearls and jewels' for his step-daughters. 'Cinderella...went to her mother's grave and planted the branch on it. ...and it grew and became a handsome tree.' And beneath this hazel tree she prayed for, and received, what was necessary for the formation of her own identity:

> 'Shiver and quiver, little tree,
> Silver and gold throw down over me.'

And she received 'gold and silver dresses' which were so 'splendid and magnificent' that 'everyone was astonished at her beauty,' and 'the king's son ...danced with no one but her. When others came and invited her, he said: "This is my partner."... As they [later] passed by the hazel-tree, it was confirmed: "That is the true bride!"' And, through the power of love, Cinderella became the queen she was born to be.

As a further amplification, the meaning of the hazel tree may be introduced. Most religions speak of a holy tree in the middle of the world. *The Old Testament*, too, mentions a 'tree in the garden...the tree in the middle of it...' (*Genesis* 3:3). Thus the message of *Cinderella* may be: learn to find the sources of life, as well as the spiritual wells, in this world. Then, symbolically speaking, man 'will not know thirst any more' (*John* 4:13).

In the continued interpretation and amplification of the Cinderella story, almost endless opportunities for talking about essential human conditions of importance for social life inside and outside the hospital appear. This may lead to a better coping with the matters of life in general and of psychic illness in particular, and, it is hoped, for many of the patients, it results in an integrated life outside the hospital after a period of time behind the protective walls of it. The chaplain has to pay supportive visits to some of these patients at certain intervals following their discharge from hospital.

The Rationale of the Choice of Fairy Tales

Being engaged in fairy tale interpretations brings about the realization that these stories reflect elements that are suitable for addressing countless affective states in man's psychic development as well as in human relations. In Jung's opinion, the collected treasure of fairy tales reflects everything that has ever taken place in the human mind from time immemorial. Consequently, the individual conversation participant may perceive *his* particular situation or actual life-problem in the course of events in the fairy tales, if these are adequately interpreted for adults. Although probably all fairy tales are suited to interpretative conversation, the narrator may want to select certain tales which are fit for special purposes; for example, for various cases of psychological disturbance.

The reason for choosing these fairy tales has been to present concerns which command attention, for example developmental conflicts (*Hänsel and Gretel, Little Snow-White, Little Briar-Rose, The Cat with the Boots*), matrimonial conflicts (*The Frog-King, or Iron-Henry*) and problems regarding personal failure, guilt, search for meaning or other aspects of coping with general life problems (*Hans in Luck, The Valiant Little Tailor* and *Cinderella*). Thus the main themes have dealt with emotional aspects of separation, anxiety and reunion; all of the aspects of life which often have become overwhelmingly significant in the lives of mentally disturbed people.

The shrewd common sense with which fairy tales deal with the practical affairs of everyday life contains flashes of insight that may enable us to solve problems and reveal to us characteristics in ourselves which surprise us. Rightly interpreted, fairy tales may thus act as a guide when we are lost in our internal bewilderment and help us overcome difficulties that have been discarded as unsolvable. Although no single fairy tale adequately explains the troubles of any single person, we will find a considerable amount of truth in all of them. For, ultimately, we are created as individuals, but as individuals who need each other.

Closing Reflections on the Epistemological Background

My personal interest in interpreting symbols in general, and interpreting symbols with patients in particular, has its origin in pastoral psychology. Pastoral psychology has for some decades been a very useful, and for me a necessary, instrument to enable me do my pastoral work in church services and personal counselling in a responsible and qualified way.

Internationally, in the Pastoral Care and Counselling Movement, the German pastoral psychologist and psychoanalyst, Joachim Scharfenberg, Professor of Practical Theology at the University of Kiel, has played a particularly inspiring role for my pastoral care and counselling endeavours. Scharfenberg's works on 'living with symbols'(Scharfenberg and Kämpfer 1980, pp.84, 104) are very helpful in coping with human conflicts. In his view, conflicts can be dealt with and solved in a constructive way if the necessary symbols are available, 'the symbol being carrier of a communicative meaning.'

Thus many neurotic and some psychotic disturbances can be avoided or cured because 'through the symbols, the diffuse world of emotions has found a language' which may convey meaning to the consciousness. The epistemological arguments for this viewpoint are elaborated on by Scharfenberg as 'identificatorial cognition through empathy' in his book *Einführung in die Pasto-*

ralpsychologie. The following brief summary gives some details of Scharfenberg's reflections on identificatorial cognition.

Making oneself acquainted with another person's feelings and putting oneself in his place is to identify with this person. A similar thing may happen with words which lead to the understanding of something from within. This is called empathy. Today we often do not realize that until about 300 years ago, the identificatorial cognition was the only kind of cognition. 'Similar matters can only be recognized by similar matters;' this used to be the method of cognition. Cognition was always a kind of re-cognition, because cognition invariably includes a personal internal experience. Therefore, the disquieting stories (filled with anxieties and strong emotions) of the ancients were told in such a way that these internal experiences were placed outside the individual field of experience. The stories took place in a superindividual world with legendary characters and gods; but in this world nobody had the slightest difficulty in recognizing themselves. From time immemorial, everything man considered vital and important was recorded and handed down in these stories called myths.

A myth is essentially a symbolic expression capable of 'verbalizing' an internal experience which otherwise cannot easily be formulated. Thus, transferring the experience to the external world, where it can be emotionally dealt with and made lucid, makes it less anxiety-provoking and therefore bearable. In an eminent way, the symbol combines internal and external experiences which, although they are different, may be united (the word 'symbol' derives from the Greek *symballein,* meaning 'throw or put together').

In order to give the further particulars of the formation of symbols and myth, we are fortunately not limited to the study of ancient texts or primitive tribes. All we have to do is to step into the bedrooms of our children. Small children develop, almost without exception, the peculiar phenomenon of being afraid of the dark when they are left alone in their beds at night. They show unmistakable signs of fear and misery, and since parents normally protect their children's room from the surrounding world, this state cannot be due to any external experience. Having developed the faculty of speech, the child will tell tales about the alarming encounters in the darkness of the night; encounters with ugly wolves, evil men, witches, ogres or whatever imaginary creatures they have in store. Regrettably, modern parents often assume that the source of the children's fear and unrest is the knowledge of such creatures. This is jumping to false conclusions. Indeed, if parents try to 'protect' their children against knowing about these creatures, they will only increase the children's *angst* as this is due to an internal experience, agitation or conflict. The imaginary creatures merely constitute attempted external projections of the child's internal distress.

When supplying the children with symbolic expressions of security and care, parents find that these symbols, whether derived from a biblical story or a fairy tale, actually have a soothing effect. Adults who have been acquainted with positive biblical or fairy tale symbols during their childhood may still take refuge in them and sense the emotions they evoke (Scharfenberg 1985, pp.18–23).

We probably all have a connection with the symbol and the myth and have needed them in the handling of our inner conflicts and contradictions. As to the relation between myth and fairy tale, the Jungian psychoanalyst Marie-Louise von Franz advocates the view that 'the fairy tale is like the sea, whereas the myths are like the waves on the sea; a fairy tale emerges from the sea and becomes a myth in a certain historical period, and it afterwards sinks into the sea again, becoming a fairy tale' (von Franz 1989, p.194). Thus Marie-Louise von Franz concludes that 'the fairy tale reflects the most simple, but at the same time the most fundamental structure of the psyche – the bare framework' (ibid).

This assumption makes the symbolic characters of the fairy tale ideal of 'identificatorial cognition'. Although the people and events mentioned in the Bible are not exclusively mythical, legendary or symbolic narrative expressions of individual or collective psychic phenomena (to a great extent there is a historical background for these people and events), the Bible, from beginning to end, is an invitation to identificatorial cognition. Combining religious education with fairy tale interpretations – as suggested in some of the previous examples of interpretation – may, therefore, be a natural element in the group conversations when the narrative interpreter is the hospital chaplain. Touching upon relevant topics, the interpreter may hint at the religious aspects. As Dillistone (1986) says:

> 'The most notable feature of the humanity [of Jesus, the principal character of *The New Testament*] was his capacity to live symbolically, to create new verbal symbols, to perform symbolic actions, to communicate with others through symbolic forms. Thus he became man, not just for a particular place Galilee, nor for a particular time early in the first century but for all places and all times, a symbolic figure, speaking and acting symbolically, and thereby standing forth as representative man, man displaying his highest and most notable quality: that of pointing beyond the direct and immediate to the transcendent and the ultimate' (p.163).

A comparison of the significant documents (including the Bible) of the ancient world shows that they all agree in distinguishing between the internal and the external worlds, but by no means do they divide them.

But with René Descartes (1596-1677) who, in his philosophical work, distinguished between the objective world (*res extensa*) and the subjective world (*res cogitans*), the two worlds are no longer connected, and the road is clear for the unscrupulous victories of the natural sciences. Despite the benefits of our technical civilization, man has begun to ask whether or not it has been a Pyrrhic victory. Actually, this, 'victory' may have devastating consequences for maintaining human sanity. Nowadays, the ability to distinguish between the two worlds has even been used as a criterion for judging mental health. Only he who clearly recognizes the distinction between subject and object is mentally sane – he who does not is out of his mind, not 'thrown or put together' (cf. *symballein*).

So far, so good. But often the spiritual values of the subjective world are ignored or even despised, resulting in dangerous suppressed complexes and a lack of symbols for diminishing 'the fear of the dark', i.e. also a lack of symbols for converting the powers in the dark – the shadows (Jung) into useful positive psychic light producing energy. Thus the psychic delusion itself is a symbolic attempt on the part of the split personality to put together a mind that has been divided for some internal or external reason because too little attention was paid to the wisdom of the Gospel: 'What God, then, has joined, let no man put asunder.' (*Matthew* 19:6).

Fairy tale conversations aim to help the patients, according to their desires and abilities in an unforced and voluntary way, to put together these divided parts; the narrative element being the core of the interpretation method. In this way, too, love can be expanded and extended between patients and members of staff so that both parties are devoted to each other. In this everybody will find their own fulfilment, and, no doubt, as long as mankind exists, we will need such combining efforts in order to counteract the psychotic transformation. Without contact with the depth of the psyche, the *Symbols of the Soul*, no man can find community with man and God, that is, meaning, because

> 'No man is an iland, intire
> of itself; every man is a peece
> of the continent, a part of
> the maine...'

John Donne, *Devotions*, 1624

CHAPTER 5

Peter Pan – The Eternally Flying Child

Birgitte Brun

Like a hook in the ocean,
sunk into the unconscious
captures dark figures repressed
images from before birth
before the first beat of your heart.
Ancient heads covered in scales
and seaweed with stone in mouth
and an unseeing look, inscrutable
between laughter and horror.
Captures dancing limbs smooth
before the fire and the night
shadows of your own self
shadows you once cast
on the wall of leaves beneath the sun in the grass
while deer stood still with quivering ears
and hooves poised between trust and flight.
Here your beginning and here your future
when you lower your forehead towards the earth
and see like the one who drinks from the river
the shadow your secret brother.

Ole Wivel (1961), translated by Else Redknap (1991)

Introduction

During psychotherapeutic work with one woman (I shall call her Ruth), it happened that she developed intense experiences of flying – imaginary, but also very vivid. She felt that her legs would rise from the ground, and it was almost as if she was carried away.

These experiences occurred when we were together, but she also described how she could feel that she was drawn towards the traffic in the streets. She was afraid that she would not be able to resist the strong pull. She feared she could be run over. This woman had had a very difficult childhood, feeling isolated and dominated by her family. At the stage in which she developed flying experiences, circumstances in her life were changing, and even if she had been longing for a change, she was, as I saw it, in an existential crisis involving her instinct of self preservation and also her libidinous drives.

At the time when this happened to the patient, I was reading the fairy tale *Peter Peter Pan and Wendy* (Barrie 1911) to my daughter. I knew the fairy tale from my own childhood, but otherwise I had not been preoccupied with it. Suddenly, it struck me that the flying fantasies, which had been so significant for Ruth, might be seen as part of a story which was also that of Peter Pan.

Although Ruth was a mature and responsible person, there were similarities with Peter Pan in the sense that neither of them really wanted to grow up. This, however, also meant that Ruth was still in contact with the child in herself. Many grown-ups have lost that feeling, which is clearly illustrated in the book, where Barrie (1911) explains what happened to the children who lived part of their childhood in Neverland.

> 'You may see the twins and Nibs and Curly any day going to an office, each carrying a little bag and an umbrella. Michael is an engine-driver, Sligtly married a lady of title, and so he became a lord. You see the judge in a wig coming out at the iron door? That used to be Tootles. The bearded man who doesn't know any story to tell his children was once John' (p.308).

To refer to John as the bearded man who was once John is a strong indication of a serious loss in identity and personality. It provides an intuitive understanding of one of the reasons why Peter Pan, and many children with him, were afraid of losing their childhood and the strong imaginary powers which characterizes this important period in life. Our thoughts, fantasies, sensations and emotions are very intense when we are children, and to grow up, gaining new territories, also implies that you have to give up something valuable.

To have a Neverland is part of the child's fantasy and inner life. So long as the child is able to leave Neverland and return to reality, Neverland can be seen as something valuable, particularly if the child is able to remember part of his private land when growing up – this often shows that he has still creative fantasies.

Peter Pan was first introduced in a novel for adults called *The Little White Bird* published in 1902. Most of the book is told by the narrator as a story to a little boy, who is addressed in the book, and one of the stories is that of Peter Pan. Barrie was a highly successful playwright when *Peter Pan* was first performed as a play in 1904 (Rose 1984). From 1911, we have the book *Peter Pan and Wendy*, to which I refer.

All his life James Barrie was faithful to the idea that he did not remember how he created the play and wrote it down. He was not able to remember, and in this way he was just like Peter Pan, who always forgets.

Barrie introduces his book about Peter Pan and Wendy as follows: 'All children, except one, grow up. They soon know that they will grow up, and the way Wendy knew was this. One day when she was two years old, she was playing in a garden, and she plucked another flower and ran with it to her mother. I suppose she must have looked rather delightful, for Mrs Darling put her hand to her heart and cried: "Oh, why can't you remain like this for ever." This was all that passed between them on the subject, but henceforth Wendy knew that she must grow up. You always know after you are two. Two is the beginning of the end' (p.11)

Through this introduction the author tells us indirectly that, in contrast to Wendy, Peter Pan never really passes the age of two. From a developmental point of view he has remained at an earlier stage. In 1911, Barrie indicated what child psychoanalytic experiences have later taught us, that sexual identity and differentiation have reached a fairly advanced stage in the normal two-year-old child. Wendy somehow knows that she will grow up and become like her mother, a grown-up woman; perhaps she has also got a vague idea that she is going to become old and die – 'Two is the beginning of the end'.

The story, you remember, starts in London. As happens in fairy tales, a partly realistic frame and many realistic details help us to keep the illusion while the imagination gains access to the story. So Kensington Gardens and its neighbourhood in London is quite a comforting place to start. The family of the story is the Darling family which has three children – Wendy, John and Michael – who fly off to Neverland with Peter Pan. Here live 'the lost boys', who fell out of their prams when their nurses, not looking after the children, were busy looking after something else. One of the many jealousy themes in the fairy tale becomes quite clear in this scene. The lost boys have been given up by their parents.

Wendy becomes a kind of mother to all the children. In his own way Peter Pan is a kind of father, even if he never accepts anything like the identity of a grown-up man, and he refuses bodily contact. Like the lost boys, Peter Pan is without parents. In Neverland the children are challenged with dangers. Peter Pan defends them, but it is characteristic that he acts without any real responsibility or emotional engagement. It says: 'He killed with a smile' and 'It was his cleverness that interested him and not the saving of human life'. The hero in a fairy tale is often described as without real feelings.

In Neverland the children meet mermaids in the lagoon, a neverbird, fairies, pirates, the crocodile that has swallowed a clock and the frightful Captain Hook. Captain Hook has lost one of his arms when fighting Peter Pan. Peter Pan always wins when he fights. One day the children return to the world of reality, where they grow up as ordinary people. As for Wendy it says: 'She was one of the kind that likes to grow up. In the end she grew up of her own free will a day quicker than other girls'. Peter Pan, however, does not want to grow up and he lives most of his time in Neverland. Now and then he will turn up to fetch Wendys's great granddaughter or great great granddaughter, just as he fetched her daughter and granddaughter, to do the spring cleaning. He does not come every year, because he is unable to keep track of time and so forgets.

The fairy tale illustrates normative developmental crisis during childhood as I shall later describe it. We gain an understanding of the precarious balance between fantasy and reality, and we follow a drama concerning life and death, progress and regression.

I thought these aspects might prove valuable in the psychotherapeutic process with Ruth. The 'flying-symptom', as it might be described, seemed difficult to deal with at first, but when we attached it to the Peter Pan figure, it became easier to handle – in a paradoxical way more realistic, but also less frightening – so when I introduced the fairy tale figure by asking Ruth 'Do you know *Peter Pan*?' she reacted spontaneously by saying: 'I love *Peter Pan*.' It came almost as a relief.

Having been preoccupied with the *Peter Pan* fairy tale and the psychoanalytic literature based on the story, I became interested in the author and his life. It was almost as if writing *Peter Pan* had been a kind of self-psychotherapy which Barrie had been through to solve some of his own problems and overcome serious traumas in his life. (At the end of this chapter I have chosen to reflect upon this theme.)

Personality Development and Developmental Crisis in *Peter Pan*

As we have already shown, we find many symbols in fairy tales centered around individuals, objects and actions. We have explored some symbols in *Peter Pan*, since they were significant in the psychotherapeutic process.

Barrie characterized Peter Pan in the following way: 'He was a lively boy, clad in skeleton leaves and the juices that ooze out of trees, but the most entrancing thing about him was that he had all his first teeth. When he saw she was a grown up (referring to Mrs Darling) he gnashed the little pearls at her.'

According to Griffith (1979, p.27), the child in the fairy tale symbolizes the unconscious and life after death. The child is dying when entering Neverland, but it may be born again. The child, which is not able to leave Neverland, is not able to achieve sexual identity. It is then fixated at a very early developmental stage, and in a way one might say the child is not alive. Peter Pan has thus been seen as an illustration of the dead child (Brun 1989).

Ralph J. Hallman (1969) focuses on the Peter Pan figure as an exemplification of the eternal child. Four constituent elements identify this figure: his abandonment, (nobody seemed to search for Peter when he ran away at seven days old), his invincibility (Peter Pan never loses a fight), his hermaphroditism (he has no clear sexual identity) and his potentiality (his magic flying powers).

When a hero's parents are hardly mentioned in a fairy tale, representations of parents will usually take more archaic shapes and thus symbolize the personality of very early life. It is said about Peter Pan that he was a smile in the corner of Mrs Darling's mouth, which almost makes you think of a woman not yet pregnant, but longing to be so in a kind of dreaming, presymbiotic stage; a paradise not yet gained.

Love and sexuality symbolize the creative union of what is in opposition to one other. This union provides the basis for new life in a child. In order to reach this stage it is necessary for the child to have grown independent of its parents. The grown-up role implies that the individual is capable of living with antagonisms and conflicts. Peter Pan has not got this kind of strength. He was not like Wendy, one of the kind that likes to grow up. He did not grow up of his own free will.

With his early developmental stagnation, the Peter Pan figure is also the androgynous existence. Let us quote from Mudd's (1990, p.130) article 'The Dark Self': 'The capacity gained at birth or at other critical points in the life cycle to face and survive the physical threat of death underlies the ability to let go, to change, and to meet destiny.'

The birth process also reminds us of Plato's image of the first humans as described by the character Aristophanes in the *Symposium*. These humans, you may recall, were round creatures with two heads and two sets of limbs who were so content within themselves they felt no need for the favour of the gods, and so neglected their obligations to make proper sacrifice. The gods in their narcissistic rage wanted to destroy them for their arrogance, but Zeus saw a more advantageous solution and decided instead to split them in half. The result, when the work of bisection was complete, left each half with a desperate yearning for the other, so that they ran towards each other and flung their arms around each others' necks and asked for nothing better than to be rolled into one, so much so that they began to die of hunger and general inertia for neither would do anything without the other. These images could, according to Mudd, just as easily depict birth trauma, and anaclitic postpartum depressions, where traumatic separation is the key feature. Traumatic separation from the mother seems part of the essence of the story of Peter Pan.

Peter Pan (Barrie, 1911, p.274) characterizes himself in the following way: 'I am youth, I am joy, I am a little bird that has come out of the egg.' Peter ran away from his home the day he was born. He could still remember how to fly because all children are birds first, we are told, and it usually takes about two years for them to become completely human which, according to modern developmental psychology, implies that the child has developed sexual identity.

A little white bird could be a dove. The dove is the bird of Venus. In alchemy it stands for the albedo signifying the individual's first clear awareness of the unconscious. The bird in fairy tales often expresses the anima, that is, the feeling and inspiration. The bird also expresses death, the soul leaving the body, so we have a close connection between birth and death in the symbol of the little white bird.

When using fairy tales in psychotherapy, one is interested in the possibilities of identification. If birth trauma and traumatic separation has, to a greater or lesser extent, been of significance for a patient in early childhood, it will be natural to identify with Peter Pan. Even if one never goes into a psychodynamic interpretation of separation conflicts in Peter Pan's life, this aspect is likely to have an unconscious influence through the symbolic value of the Peter Pan figure. Sometimes it is easier to make contact with essential feelings and longings through the symbols in fairy tales than to work more directly with the patient's associations, as we have already described. And you can always withdraw from Peter Pan – after all he is 'just gay and innocent and heartless'.

If, in psychotherapy, one is dealing with disturbances from very early childhood, at a time when the child was not yet able to speak, visual experiences and images seem to be valuable. We see the world around us before we are able to talk about it. Peter Pan is a strong visual symbol, helping the patient to get in contact with very early and basic feelings, for which there existed no words. His immortality and eternal childhood, his failing memory and his inability to feel guilt and responsibility, can be looked upon as the expression of a developmental arrest. In the psychotherapeutic process, he helps us to get down to bodily sensations, somatic intuition – 'a bodily knowledge or awareness of the presence and possibility of death that promotes an ever-increasing awareness of separation between ego and self and between child and parent' (Mudd 1990, p.131).

What do we know about the identity of Peter Pan through his name and its symbolic implications? Barrie may have thought of Peter Davies, the youngest of the three Davies boys he was concerned about (Blake 1977). What we realise is that it is much shorter than Wendy's long, impressive name Wendy Moyra Angela Darling, of which she is very proud. 'Peter' is a Christian name and one might suggest that Peter is the divine and innocent child. The name 'Pan' makes us think of the god of the shepherds from Arcadia, half buck with a human body, goat legs and horns on his forehead. He is kind, helpful, gay – but also he is dangerous. When a quiet herd of cattle would suddenly jump up and rush off, the ancient Greek herdsmen thought it was Pan at work. He made the cattle get into a panic, and people too could be struck by panic.

Peter Pan is closely related to his pipes, and here we have another motif which attaches him to the Pan figure. Pan plays the pipes, and he chases the nymphs. His pipe is a transformed nymph. The story goes that Zeus saved the nymph from Pan's advances by transforming her into a bullrush. Out of the bullrush Pan cut his pipe. Bearing in mind Pan and his pipe, Peter Pan contains masculine and feminine characteristics. Pan is the god of the woods. His mother, who was a nymph, rejected him because she became afraid of his appearance. The Greek god Pan has given features to Satan, who is often pictured with horns and legs from a goat and is represented as ithyphallic (Nyborg 1962). Pan's father was Hermes, who followed the dead as shades to Hades. Hermes has given the name to the concept *hermaphrodite*, which leads to associations to the androgynous existence already described as characteristic of the Peter Pan figure.

Peter is the light side and Pan the dark side of the figure. The name 'Peter Pan' expresses a conflict between good and evil, life and death, or a union – part of the boy is alive and part of him is dead. One psychotic man who changed his name quite frequently in his search for identity, chose a forename that included a strongly confirming word and a surname which was characterized by negation. In this way he fought for completion, and also, as I saw it, to avoid taking responsibility.

From *The Old Testament* we have the image of Eve created out of Adam's rib, and it is *Genesis* we think of when Wendy says to Peter Pan: 'I know such lots of stories,' and the author continues: 'So there can be no denying that it was she who first tempted him'.

In his description of Peter Pan the author emphasized that Peter is exactly Wendy's size in mind and body, so the two figures are closely attached to each other. Looking at the child couple Peter Pan and Wendy, you also find an illustration of the androgynous (the double-sexed) existence of ancient origin; the symbol of the unity of personality called the self. In man's psyche it is consciousness that has masculine features, whereas the unconscious has a feminine quality. In the play *Peter Pan*, the undifferentiated in the sexual identity is emphasized because the role of Peter Pan was written for an actress and was thus performed by a woman.

The next developmental phase with its crisis, as illustrated in the story is the Oedipal phase. Wendy is disappointed with her father Mr Darling, who is immature, self centred and weak. The relationship with her mother (described as wonderful), becomes difficult because her mother is superficial and simultaneously controlling and domineering. Meisel (1977) tends to see Wendy's flight with Peter Pan to Neverland against this background. In relation to this interpretation Peter Pan can be looked upon as Wendy's imaginary friend.

Following Wendy we also get a rich illustration of jealousy problems in a girl born in England just around the year 1900, closely followed by two boys who, to use Barrie's expression 'if not favoured, at least enjoy the special extra pomp that was due to the birth of a male'. When using *Peter Pan* in psychotherapy Wendy is an important guide, whether one talks about her or not, since her relationship with Peter Pan is very close, and she does not lose a sense of reality. She never loses her perspective of time.

Peter Pan puts aside ideas about what it would be like to have an adult, masculine sexual identity. When Wendy imagines the two as a couple, Peter Pan reacts by rejecting and avoiding these ideas. He can never pass and reach beyond the love you may feel in relation to a sister or a mother, and this love is also limited by his inability to create continuity in his experiences. Peter Pan denies the beginning of the end.

When Wendy asks: 'What are your exact feelings for me?' Peter Pan answers 'those of a devoted son'. Characteristic is the following dialogue:

> **PETER:** I don't want to be a man. O Wendy's mother, if I was to wake up and feel there was a beard.
>
> **WENDY:** I should love you in a beard.
>
> **PETER:** Keep back, lady, no one is going to catch me and make me a man
>
> (Barrie 1911).

The next developmental phase that it is natural to work with in relation to Peter Pan is the latency age. This is a period in childhood where the child is able to take increasing responsibility, identifying with the adults, and the learning potential in the healthy, active child is tremendous. As for Peter Pan, we realize that he keeps his first teeth, and it is said of him: 'For one thing he despised all mothers except Wendy, and for another, he was the only boy on the island who could neither write nor spell, not the smallest word. He was above all that sort of things.' Peter Pan is fixated at the oedipal psycho-developmental stage, and he is not able to enter the latency age, which requires hard work and, for a boy, also masculine identity. His intellectual drives are disturbed.

According to theories of developmental psychology, at around six years the child will often have fantasies about running away. The travel to Neverland thus illustrates the wish to run away, become independent and free from parents' influence. It is also running away from the increasing demands on the growing child to take still more responsibility, a developmental crisis – just as we see it with Pinocchio, who would not go to school (Lorenzini 1883).

Peter Pan fights Captain Hook and the pirates. As for the pirates, we hear them before they are seen, and it is always the same dreadful song:

> 'Avast belay, yo ho, heave to,
> A-pirating we go,
> And if we're parted by a shot
> We're sure to meet below' (Barrie 1911).

The pirates could be seen as aggression, and thus as destructive forces, which are also frightening and could lead to death. Part of the drama in the story concerns the fighting between Peter Pan and Captain Hook, who wants Wendy for himself. This fighting is characteristic of the oedipal phase – we use the expression oedipal rivalry. It is important for the boy not to beat his father, since this will protect him from getting too close to his mother. At the same time it is important for him to identify with his father as part of his masculine identity development. In puberty, a new fight is taking place.

The child listening to the story, identifying with Peter Pan, is keen to see Peter beating Captain Hook; but we look upon the destruction of Captain Hook in a different way. In puberty, the boy will normally enter a new kind of rivalry with his father through the difficult process of becoming a man and developing his own individual personality. Part of this development is showing courage and increasing responsibility, as illustrated in the story of Pinocchio (Collodi 1920), when he rescues his old father from the shark. A father should not try to compete with his young son (as some fathers actually do). What the son needs is a careful balance between consideration and challenge from a father who loves him and is ready to see him as a self-reliant, confident and responsible young man who is gradually becoming stronger than himself.

Being in the power of the negative feminine, Peter Pan fights Captain Hook, so that the fighting is not part of a positive masculine identity development, with grown-up men to imitate and identify with. Winning the fight and dressing up in Captain Hook's wickedest garments seems to show an identification process that has failed, and thus developmental arrest. Wendy somehow realizes this, and Peter's dressing up in Captain Hook's clothes is much against her will.

There are two father figures in the story – Mr Darling and Captain Hook. In many fairy tales we have the good mother in the grave and the wicked step-mother very much alive (as in *Cinderella*). No doubt Captain Hook is a wicked and destructive father figure who has still got the boarding-school boy in him, which shows his immaturity. As for Mr Darling, he is very kind, but also very weak, so he is not a good father to identify with either. Barrie decided that the two should be acted by the same actor, which illustrates that they are parts of the same figure.

In Neverland all traces disappear into oblivion. The small elf Tinker Bell is close to Peter Pan always. She has very strong feelings, and quite easily becomes jealous of Wendy – 'You are a great ugly girl' is her very illustrative expression of her feelings. Tinker Bell is characterized as being all bad or all good. 'Fairies have to be one thing or the other, because being so small, unfortunately they only have room for one feeling at a time.' Thus we see that Tinker Bell symbolizes strong, nonconflicting feelings, again belonging to an early developmental phase. It is part of growing up to be able to contain ambivalent and conflicting feelings; but, being very small, you have only room for one feeling at a time.

In Neverland there are mermaids, and the title of Chapter III, where the children fly to Neverland, is 'Come away, come away'. Before looking at the significance of this strange and somehow contradictory title we will look at the significance of Neverland – originally Never Never Neverland.

In fairy tales an island is often a place where creatures live that belong to another world. The island has assimilated projections from the unconscious. Some islands are for the dead. In the unconscious sea, the island represents a separation from the conscious psyche. von Franz (1987) points out that the island in the ocean is often a symbol of isolation. It is generally a magical realm inhabited by otherworldly figures.

Griffith (1979) suggests that Neverland, 'the map of a person's mind', is an ambiguous place. One part of the psyche desires and therefore creates it; another part denies and retreats from it, insisting that it is only make-believe when it threatens to become too real for the imagination. Thus Neverland is also an illustration of the danger of the unconscious gaining control and overwhelming the whole personality, as it is seen in psychoses. To help psychotics sometimes one has to travel to Neverland, because that is where they are. If you manage to travel so far, you try to gain access to the island. Sometimes the journey is quite long, and you are not always fortunate enough to have Peter Pan or a fairy as a guide. Besides, it requires courage, somehow, to set free what is otherwise controlled in yourself. When you are in Neverland, you will try to meet the person you are looking for, showing him ways back – if he lets you.

In *Peter Pan* it is said: 'When you play it by day with the chairs and table-cloth, it is not in the least alarming, but in the two minutes before you go to sleep, it becomes very nearly real. That is why there are night-lights.'

Chapter III of the book has the strange title 'Come away, come away'. It seems tempting, but also frightening. In Brøndsted's book *The Mermaids' Saga* (1965) I found a means of understanding this. There is an old Cornish myth that ends with Walter going down to the beach. The night is dark, full of stars. He hears a voice which he has heard before: 'Join all hands, might and main. Weave the sands, form a chain, He, my lover, comes again.' This is repeated by a large choir. He continues on his way and is received by Selina with wild laughter. She is Selina, but yet not her; she is a mermaid inside. She kisses Walter. 'You are mine to death.' For hours she kisses, but the water rises and the heavens get dark. 'Give me back the dead', she said. His fright and pain was great, the waters rose, there was thunder. A huge wave carried him and the girl away. She held him by the hair singing:

> 'Come away, come away, o'er the waters wild.
> Our earth-born child
> Died this day, died this day.'

Thousands of voices come from mermaids – they were tossing the dying Walter, whose false heart thus endured the vengeance of the mermaid, who had, through fondness of heart, made the innocent child of humble parents the child of her adoption (Brøndsted 1965, p.123–124).

'Come away' is the introduction to Neverland and, so it seems, also to thoughts about death; an unreal existence. We realize that Peter Pan avoided bodily contact; somehow it seemed frightening, almost as in Walter's song. We also realize that Peter Pan forgets everything. Nyborg (1962) explains how bodily contact such as a kiss can have magic power resulting in forgetting. In Hans Christian Andersen's fairy tale *The Snow Queen*, The Queen kisses Kay twice, but leaves out the third kiss, 'Now you get no more kisses,' she says, 'Because otherwise I shall kiss you to death.' Kay enters another world when he loses contact with reality. His situation, says Nyborg, illustrates the fact that he is possessed by an archetype; the Snow Queen is the devil's partner. The loss

of memory that characterizes Peter Pan may be due to the influer
negative aspects of the mother-archetype, which results in devel
arrest. Barrie was a highly educated man and is likely to have been fam
Cornish mythology, just as he was familiar with Greek mythology.

During the psychotherapeutic process, Ruth sometimes expressed ambivalent feelings. She wished that I would offer her bodily contact, as a mother would
her child, but she was also frightened that I should do so. Apart from the
complicated aspects of positive and negative transference and countertransference in this situation, I felt that her fright had to do with fighting regression,
which is a continual fight in childhood, and one which is very clearly illustrated
in *Peter Pan*.

The Shadow Motif in Peter Pan

In *Peter Pan and Wendy*, Peter Pan comes to the Darling family at the beginning
of the story because he has lost his shadow. He tries to fix it with soap, but in
vain. At last Wendy helps him by sowing his shadow to his heel.

Fraser (1976) argues that primitive man often regards his shadow as a
reflection of his soul, or of a vital part of himself; as such it is necessarily a source
of danger to him. For if it is trampled upon, struck or stabbed, he will feel the
injury as if it were done to his person, and if it is detached from him entirely (as
he believes it is possible for it to be) he will die. So the shadow motif has to do
with the feeling of bodily integrity and the anxiety in the child concerning bodily
harm. It has to do with sexuality and fantasies, and feelings related to sexual
activities.

Wharton (1990) explains the archetypal numinosity of the shadow, the
feeling that the shadow belongs to oneself, as a kind of elusive 'double', which
expresses or reflects oneself but in a mirror-image, through which one can be
hurt or damaged. He sees the shadow as an essential part of a person's identity
and being. Becoming detached from one's shadow means being unconscious of
it. People may suppress the awareness of 'two-ness' in themselves, the duality,
the conflict between what they would like to be and what they are. We sometimes want to live in a preambivalent, illusory world, in which life would be
simple, all-good, blissfully free of conflict. In his article 'The hidden face of
shame' Wharton (1990) writes:

> 'I remember one game that involved trying to tread on someone else's
> shadow, which would then mean that the person was "dead", but at the
> same time avoiding having one's own shadow trodden on. If it was
> trodden on, the feeling was that it might become trapped and detached
> like Peter Pan's shadow' (p.280).

Asper (1989), looking at shadow aspects of narcissistic disorders, has expressed
the 'shadow-complex' in the following way: 'True, whoever looks into the
mirror of the water will see first his own face. Whoever goes to himself risks a

confrontation with himself. The mirror does not flatter. It faithfully shows whoever looks into it, namely the face we never show to the world because we cover it with the persona, the mask of the actor. But the mirror lies behind the mask and shows the true face'

The shadow in *Peter Pan* is easily associated with the shadow-idea described by Jung. The shadow in his theory belongs partly to the personal and partly to the collective unconscious. Nyborg (1962) gives a clear description of Jung's idea. 'It is an archetypal figure, which we meet like our alter-ego. It represents our undeveloped characteristics – good as well as bad, all that which we are also. It represents a piece of life in us, which has not been lived. It represents talents in us, which have not been expressed. The shadow is always, where the ego is not. Together they form the sum of our psychic possibilities' (p.34).

Nyborg uses the expression 'our internal double-personality', and he emphasizes that if we could face our own envy, viciousness and our hate, then we could use these sides positively, because there is so much life in such destructive feelings. If all this energy was at our disposal, it could be applied in a positive way. The confrontation with the shadow-aspects of our personalities is essential in psychotherapy, even if it is very difficult and takes a long time.

It is an interesting reflection that the devil does not throw a shadow: he is immortal. According to Greek mythology, the dead living in Hades are not real people, but live a life in which there is no change and no development. If Peter Pan loses his shadow he will die, no longer being able to return to life – not even as an onlooker.

If you think of your shadow, you will probably have the feeling that you are the master, in the sense that *you* are the one to decide where to go, not the other way round; but in Hans Christian Andersen's fairy tale *The Shadow* (1966) the roles have changed – the Shadow takes control of its master.

There are similarities in these stories between Peter Pan and the Shadow. The Shadow, it is told by Andersen, travels on his own and, returning to the learned man, tells that he has been away for three weeks, 'and it means as much as living for three thousand years and reading all that man has imagined and written down.' It is an imaginary world described here, with quite a different time-perspective from that of the real world. It makes us think of Neverland.

On his travels, the Shadow meets a princess. In the end, she becomes his bride, while the learned man is put to death. The princess hears that the Shadow has come to make his beard grow, but the princess thinks she knows the real reason. He cannot throw a shadow. She says: 'I do hope his beard won't grow, because then he would be off at once.' This reaction is different from Wendy's – Wendy would love to see Peter Pan with a beard. Wendy keeps in touch with the real world, whereas the princess in *The Shadow* is just as unreal as The Shadow. 'She was light enough, but he was still lighter,' and 'she could very nearly see through him.' Obviously, growing a beard has to do with masculine identity and sexuality, which can be a difficult and sometimes anxiety-provoking process. It can also mean that you lose your ability to fantasize, as happened to John, who was not able to tell his children any stories when he became a man with a beard.

The window motif, and peeping in at the windows, is also something which Peter Pan and the Shadow have in common. The princess in *The Shadow* dances with the shadow. 'She told him the country she came from. He knew it, and had been there while she was away, he had peeped in at the windows on every floor, and seen all sorts of things through them.' In *Peter Pan* the chapter 'The Return Home' ends like this: 'There could not have been a lovelier sight, but there was none to see it except a strange boy who was staring in at the window. He had ecstasies innumerable that other children can never know, but he was looking through the window at the one joy from which he must be for ever barred' (p.295). The Shadow and Peter Pan could see many things, but they were there as unlookers not as participants.

The shadow concept is linked with feelings of guilt and shame. Shame, according to Wharton (1990), has two aspects: a defensive and an affective experience. Erikson (1968) has suggested that the child is susceptible to shame at around the age when it learns to stand upright and to walk. At this stage the child gains an increased awareness of its own relative smallness, helplessness, and potential for failure. The feeling of shame experienced at this very early stage in life can be there to disturb later development.

Feeling unloved, indeed unlovable, is the essence of shame as it is found in the narcissistically wounded person. The omnipotent wish to fly may help to restore your hurt feelings. Feelings of shame, which are very basic and early experiences have been retained in our bodies and souls but, being such early experiences, are difficult to express in words; again, Peter Pan can be helpful.

Peter Pan and the Psychotherapeutic Process

It can be a relief to the patient in psychotherapy to regress to earlier developmental stages, if the regression does not get out of control. As for Ruth, her flying experiences were related to wishes and longings going back to a very early period in her life – it seemed almost back to prenatal existence. As part of the transference during the psychotherapeutic process, she longed for close contact with me. These feelings were positive and exciting, but also frightening and strange to her. She expressed fantasies in which we were both flying. Having introduced Peter Pan, as I did in this period, he became a transitional object, which made her feel safer. We talked about his anxiety concerning growing up, his flight to Neverland and about him missing his mother, even if he would never admit it. In this way we could gradually approach memories about her mother and the almost bodily feeling of being rejected which she had felt from her father during childhood.

During the period in which we worked with Peter Pan, she made herself a dress, which we never talked about; but I saw it as a Peter Pan dress. I also saw the little girl trying to make contact with her mother, and I saw her striving to make contact with a distant and very introvert father. In *Peter Pan* the small boy gains control over his father and wins the oedipal fight. This is not healthy because it disturbs his opportunities of identifying with his father, and it implies that he gets too closely attached to his mother, almost taking his father's place. As for the little girl, she should not take her mother's place in her relationship with her father. But it is very important that she has the feeling of being loved; after all, the father is the first man in a girl's life and therefore very important also for the development of her sexual identity.

Peter Pan is a story about the child's imaginary world, the dream about Paradise and the difficult process of becoming independent in relation to your mother. *Peter Pan* is also the story of the tremendous power of the unconscious. It is an illustration of regression, which means going back to an earlier developmental stage instead of repressing anxiety-provoking experiences. It tells us about the difficult process of achieving sexual differentiation and sexual identity, and it is an existential story concerning life and death.

Following the development of Peter Pan and Wendy, I found it easier to see and understand important developmental aspects of the patient's life. Peter Pan became part of our mutual world. Talking about Peter Pan and Neverland, his fairyland, we could approach Ruth's fantasies about the Garden of Eden, where the relationship with her mother had been close and uncomplicated, and we could talk about her early emotional frustrations in relation to her.

Peter Pan gave us the chance to approach an understanding based on two different backgrounds. She had her images and memories and I had mine. Even if I never talked about my experience with the story, they were, no doubt, important in creating the atmosphere which facilitated our work. With *Peter Pan* between us, some of her experiences became less strange and mysterious, and confrontations in the psychotherapeutic process were not so direct and no longer so frightening. At the same time, there was a common field of experience for the patient and her psychotherapist. In this way Ruth's strange experiences could, from her point of view, be seen as part of her growing up through all the years from childhood to adult life. Somehow *Peter Pan* had a reassuring effect on both of us.

Ruth knew Peter Pan from the Walt Disney production, and it was the pictures of the figure which she was familiar with rather than the words. This is important to emphasize, since so many of the things she said and expressed in the paintings that illustrated her work with Peter Pan were close to the actual story.

In fairy tales there is the very personal and individual, but also that which is part of human life. Bettelheim (1976) suggests that this is essential to the enchantment of fairy tales. In fairy tales everything can happen. In this way fairy tale communication gives freedom to the patient and also to the psychotherapist.

Wendy may have reacted against her weak father when she flew away from her home, and Ruth had reacted with sadness and loneliness when her father was not able to meet her emotional needs. Her mother had once told her that she felt very well when she was pregnant, and that the birth of her daughter had been a happy event, but she had also felt sorry because she knew it would be her last child; she would never become pregnant again. In Neverland, Michael objects because he is kept in a cot, but Wendy answers: 'I must have somebody in a cradle, and you are the littlest. A cradle is such a nice homely thing to have about a house.'

Ruth had a remarkable memory and she still remembered the time when she was about thirteen months old and took her first steps. She had a strong inner picture of her mother's face when she managed to get up. She sees her mother's face very serious and somehow expressing sorrow. With her first steps she was on her way to two years old – 'Two is the beginning of the end'. We remember Mrs Darling's reflections concerning Wendy in the garden picking flowers; her wish that she should never change. The first steps are a strong indication of the child's gradually growing independence.

I looked on Ruth's flying fantasies as expressing her wishes to go back in time, to regress. She made a picture in silk of a small girl with a balloon and a butterfly. She named it faith, hope and love. The girl was wearing a skirt, which was pink (the small girl – of Wendy as a grown up woman it says: 'Wendy was married in white with a pink sash') and on top of it was a black skirt, which I saw as an illustration of the sexual grown up woman, and also as the theme of death; thus anxiety was in the picture. A long time after she had made the picture she told me that it was fortunate I had not touched the girl, because she would not have accepted that. I thought of Wendy in the play. She was not allowed to touch Peter Pan, (Barrie would not accept that) and I wondered whether this situation had helped me to do the right thing, if it had been an unconscious thread of guidance.

I am pretty sure that I did not think of the parallel, when I was in the situation, but it may have had an influence even so. Touching could have something to do with being in touch with the child in yourself, and this may provoke fears of helplessness and of shame. Wharton (1990) explains that in psychotherapy we try to provide an environment in which it is safe enough for the patient to experience his helplessness, and we have to be careful not to bring disturbance into this.

Later, Ruth talked about the girl as symbolizing the body, the balloon the womb, and the butterfly love. The balloon as the flying object being associated with the womb put her flying fantasies in a developmental perspective.

In psychotherapy, as part of a positive transference, patients may develop wishes and fantasies concerning close bodily contact with the psychotherapist.

These fantasies often seem related to a very early period in their lives. Some-times these wishes are followed by anxiety, anger and frustration and the negative transference will dominate. It can be a very precarious balance to work with these themes. If the patient gets too embarrassed or feels humiliated, it may have a harmful effect rather than facilitating growth. However, I have found that the fairy tale can be a kind of protection, even if you don't mention it just at that stage. From *Peter Pan* I shall quote: 'It was Wendy's custom to take him out of bed and sit with him on her lap, soothing him in dear ways of her own invention, and when he grew calmer to put him back to bed, before he quite woke up, so that he should not know of the indignity to which she had subjected him' (p.234)

If the mother has not been able to contain the child's overwhelming emo-tions, the result may be that the person has blocked off large areas of emotional experiences or he may not trust himself to express them in verbal terms. Working with Ruth, her imaginary – in many ways poetic – world and her flying fantasies, it was natural to think of the Russian-French painter Marc Chagall in whose work the motif of flying has been expressed with so many facets. On one occasion we both thought of him, since Ruth brought a postcard she had received with a Chagall-like motif, and since Chagall was brought into the room, I felt pretty sure that there would be more similarities between Peter Pan, Ruth and Chagall than the flying motif as such.

Zeiler (1986), who has been interested in the great painter's personality writes: 'Chagall was very much against learning, when he was a child. He has expressed it in this way: "I will remain untamed and wild, covered by leaves, I will scream, cry and pray." "Well Chagall," says the teacher "will you declare the lesson of today?" I started tata-ta. It felt like being thrown down from the fourth floor' (p. 1131). Later he writes: 'I was anxious about my future puberty years, anxious just to think of the slightest approach to becoming a grown-up person, anxious to grow a beard;' almost the words from Peter Pan. In such anxious depressive hours Chagall would lie under the sofa-table imagining that he was flying over the roofs.

As for Ruth, she had dreams and fantasies about wedding flowers changing into flowers put on a tomb, fantasies about a union with a mother which were related to rebirth and death, where you followed the fantasies in movements from the womb to heaven very like the imaginary world of Chagall.

Towards the end of her flying period, she presented me with a small pottery figure, which illustrates a child of about a year old stepping out of an egg-shell. This figure symbolized her own development, and she continued to work with the theme: 'I am a little bird that has broken out of the egg' says Peter Pan. The egg and the small child is also seen as a symbol of the self, the beginning of growth and development.

When the chapter in psychotherapy which one might call *Peter Pan* had finished, Ruth made a picture of Peter Pan in his green garments. A couple is seen, not quite clearly drawn; in the right corner you see Tinker Bell, or rather just a pair of red boots with laces formed almost like a pair of glasses. The painting was an illustration from a dream ending with Ruth telling Tinker Bell: 'Leave me alone. I know very well you are there.' Tinker Bell is closely associated with jealousy themes. You remember her saying to Wendy: 'You are a great ugly girl.' Jealousy themes had been worked through, but of course they don't quite disappear. Tinker Bell's red boots were quite solid, suggesting perhaps that Ruth was ready to land, just as had been the case with Wendy. When later we talked about the Peter Pan period, Ruth would characterize it as somehow magic. She expressed the wish that some magic should remain for ever.

Aspects of the Author's Story

Hermes was the father of Pan and James M. Barrie was the father of Peter Pan – that is, his author. The story of his authorship and his biography is given in Morris Fraser's book *The Death of Narcissus* in the chapter 'Soap and Shadow' (1976) and also in Jacqueline Rose's book *The Case of Peter Pan* (1984).

James M. Barrie was born in Scotland on 9 May 1860. He was part of a large family dominated by girls. He had a brother, David, seven years older, who was killed in a skating accident when he was thirteen years old. At this time Barrie was six years old. He had thus reached the age that, we must assume, is also the age of Peter Pan, since it is emphasized many times that Peter Pan never gets his real teeth.

When David died his mother, Margaret Ogilvie, reacted with such deep sorrow that she stayed in bed for weeks, perhaps even months, during which time she could do nothing. She lay hugging the christening robe. Each of her children had worn this robe when they were christened. James often looked into her room, and then withdrew and sat on the staircase outside her door crying. He often knocked on his mother's locked door in vain, while she lay in bed hugging the christening robe in her arms and longing for her dead son.

James' older sister Jane Ann broke the isolation one day by pushing James into the bedroom, encouraging him to call attention to his presence and asking his mother if she had forgotten that she had other children. With her face turned away his mother reacted by asking 'Is it you?' Barrie thought that she asked for her dead child, and he answered as he has written himself 'In a little lonely voice, "No, it no' him, it's just me." Then I heard a cry, and my mother turned in bed, and though it was dark, I knew that she was holding out her arms.'

Barrie wrote about this episode: 'I was breathing hard, or perhaps I was crying.' Many years later he wrote in *Peter Pan*: 'It is a saying in the Neverland that every time you breathe a grown-up dies.' It is easy to identify with the small James fearing to lose his mother completely.

In Neverland he is protected against sorrow, wants and guilt feelings, and he is protected against all dangers connected with aggressive impulses, since he will always win a fight, and he is not really emotionally involved when fighting. But Captain Hook had the forename James, just like Barrie, and thus you get a vague feeling of the author's anger and despair, which may have been related to the loss of his brother.

In the time to come, his mother would talk to James about her dead son, and James reacted to this by trying to become like David. He tried to make his mother forget her loss; he imitated the dead brother, identifying with him, and perhaps now and then, one might almost see a fusion, where it was difficult for him to keep his own identity separated from his brother's. David had a characteristic way of whistling, and would often stand with his legs apart and his hands in his pockets. After some practising, James could whistle like his brother. One day James dressed up secretly in a suit belonging to his dead brother. It was dark gray with small dots. Dressed in his brother's clothes James managed to get into his mother's room without her noticing. '"Listen," I cried in a glow of triumph, and I stretched my legs wide apart and plunged my hands into the pockets of my knickerbockers, and began to whistle.'

It is hardly necessary to say that it gave his mother a serious shock to see James in David's clothes, but this, however, did not disrupt the strong emotional attachment between mother and son that lasted for 29 years – the rest of Margaret Ogilvie's life. She died the same year as her daughter Jane Ann, who took care of James when David died. That year, 1894, in which Barrie reached the age of 35, he married. The marriage lasted for fifteen years. It was never consummated.

Griffith (1979) writes: 'In Barrie's mind, the issue of whether to fly away or stay at home was really settled before the story ever began. Any biography of him shows that the idea of ever really detaching himself from his home and mother would have been unbearable. His imagination had committed itself absolutely to the image of the faithful child who would remain sheerest game and make-believe... In the Neverland there exists for him another-wife figure whom he can't, even there, embrace and a villain of a father he can slay. Such visions were very likely too frightening for him to stand by, so that as soon as he hinted at them he had to repudiate them. And since he could neither fulfil them nor get rid of them he was immobilized' (p.29).

Barrie's inspiration to write came from the contact with his mother. She told him about her own childhood and many other things in the years after she had lost her eldest son. The attachment between these two was so strong that Marietta Karpe (1956) has described it almost as a psychotherapeutic process with strong transference and countertransference phenomena. Barrie himself has expressed it in this way: 'I soon grow tired of writing tales unless I can see a little girl of whom my mother has told me, wandering confidently through the pages' (Griffith 1979, p.30).

Through *Peter Pan* Barrie expresses more disturbing feelings, first by letting Peter Pan fly to Neverland – a world away from the influence of his mother, and yet not quite, since he gets hold of Wendy. We hear of Peter Pan that he could do very well without a mother. 'He had thought them out, and remembered only their bad points'. At the end of the story when he returns to the Darling family it says 'I came back for my mother, to take her back to the Neverland.' 'He does so need a mother,' the new little girl Jane says. 'Yes, I know,' Wendy admitted rather forlornly, 'no one knows it so well as I.'

It is strange to think that the author forgot all about the creative process leading to the play *Peter Pan*. In the dedication of *Peter Pan* he writes 'some disquieting confessions must be made in printing at last the play of *Peter Pan*, among them this, that I have no recollection of having written it,' and later: 'I cannot remember doing it. I remember writing the story of Peter and Wendy many years after the production of the play, but I might have copied that from some typed copy. I can haul back to mind the writing of almost every other essay of mine, however forgotten by the pretty public, but this play of Peter, no.' Barrie was ambidextrous. He has said that he wrote the most sinister things with his left hand, thus also the dedication to the play.

In the story, Peter Pan comes flying through a window, and in this way gets in touch with the Darling family for the first time. According to Karpe's interpretation, the window is connected with thoughts about death, a theme which turns up often in Barrie's works. She considers children flying through the window during the night in their nightclothes to be dead children.

Peter Pan refers to himself as a little white bird. In mythology, the dead soul leaves the body in the shape of a bird. In certain villages in Ober Wallis, you can still find a small window in the parents' bedroom. This window, according to von Franz (1987), is called the window of the soul. It is only open when someone is dying, to let the soul flow out through it.

In *Peter Pan* the father figure is either very weak (like Mr Darling) or wicked (like Captain Hook), and Peter Pan wins in the oedipal rivalry, destroying Captain Hook, which means that his masculine identity development becomes seriously disturbed and he regresses to an early developmental phase, becoming dependent on his mother. The whole fairy tale illustrates his fight for freedom – a theme that seems to have been of importance in relation to Barrie's own life. In the book, Peter Pan's arrival is described as follows: 'He was accompagnied by a strange light. Neverland had come too near. A strange boy had broken through from it.'

Barrie wrote the play *Mary Rose* in 1924. A mother returns from the grave and does not recognize her now grown up son, who has become a soldier. She sits on his lap and asks him for permission to play like a child, until he puts her to sleep. Barrie has said that his most important activity in life was to play hide and seek with the angels. The mother who wants to play on her son's lap gives a strong picture of the insufficient separation between generations, which we often meet among sensitive and disturbed people today. As a schizophrenic man expressed it: 'I had to be my mother's husband.'

Mary Rose like *Peter Pan* presents us with the theme of disappearance, this time of an eleven year old girl (the developmental phase just before puberty, late latency). Many years later she disappears again; while she is away time stands still.

The Danish author Christian Braad Thomsen (1990) who has written about the film director Alfred Hitchcock has called attention to 'the Mary Rose theme' in Hitchcock's film *Vertigo*. He writes: 'It is not hard to understand why Hitchcock was so fascinated with the Mary Rose theme. With its peculiar poetry, it is about a girl losing her way just before puberty, and about a boy who loses his mother just before the oedipal age. This is why he is able to keep a picture of her, which is not disturbed by the changes of life, like a fairy who will return one day and become united with him again as young as when she left him.'

Hitchcock had wanted to make a film about Mary Rose – the woman who, according to Thomsen, is mother and lover at the same time and therefore not possible to reach except in fantasy. She seemed to illustrate a deep trauma in Hitchcock's life, and an essential conflict in the child's development. Hitchcock has expressed the essence of the project: 'If the dead persons returned, what would we then put up with them.' It was a great disappointment to Hitchcock that at the height of his career he got no support to make the film *Mary Rose*.

Why did Barrie repress everything about the creation of Peter Pan? How did it happen that, like his hero, he has forgotten everything? Maybe part of the explanation is that Barrie, from the age of six and for the rest of his life, had had to fight against an insuperable rival to achieve his mother's love. You can feel anger towards a living father and later, perhaps, identify with him. But how can you cope with a dead brother who is older than you and has such a strong influence on your mother? The Peter Pan figure combines the dead brother, who never grows up, his mother (since the role was written for a woman) and finally, himself. Everything, in the body of a charming careless boy, who has won the hearts of millions of people; this is Karpe's interpretation.

Peter Pan would forget that time was passing by and everything changing, and the author's very strong repression, bordering on denial, provides associations to imaginary companions from the early years in childhood in normal children and in some sensitive grown up people who feel that the imaginary figures, which they themselves have created, live an independent life. Perhaps Peter Pan was an imaginary companion to Barrie. He was familiar with Peter Pan, but from where he came and how he turned up, he could not remember clearly, just as we, having reached the adult years, may be unable to explain, how an imaginary friend appeared in our early childhood.

Barrie's traumatic experience at the age of six of losing his brother, who was not yet a man and the contact with his mother, reminds one of the discoverer of Troy, Heinrich Schliemann. Niederland (1962) analyzes the life of Heinrich Schliemann: 'Schliemann grew up "The cemetery before our door" – the questions of birth, death, being alive or buried and dead, never lost their urgent, infantile puzzling character for him' (p.7).

Schliemann was born shortly after the oldest child of the family, a brother by the name of Heinrich, had died at the age of eight. The new arrival was named Heinrich after the one who had just died. Schliemann was never fully sure whether he was the dead brother inside or the living one outside the grave. He had to prove he was the latter throughout life. His identity-fusion had many similarities with Barrie's.

So far as we know, Barrie and Freud did not know one another. However, Freud was a great admirer of Schliemann, and Freud's interest in antiquities is well known. In *A Life for our Time* (1988) Gay quotes what Freud had told his friend Ferenzi: 'As he studied his prized possessions he found "Strange secret yearning" rising up in him, "Perhaps from my ancestors' heritage for the East and the Mediterranean and for a life of quite another kind, wishes from the childhood never to be fulfilled and not adapted to reality."' Freud admired Heinrich Schliemann 'that celebrated digger and discoverer of Troy's mysterious, myth-laden antiquities.' He wrote about Schliemann 'There is happiness only as fulfilment of a child's wish.' According to Gay 'It was precisely the kind of wish that Freud felt in his mournful moods, had so rarely become reality in his own life.'

CHAPTER 6

Pinocchio as a Helper in Psychotherapy
Personality Development in Pictures and Words

Marianne Runberg and Birgitte Brun

Introduction

On the 3 March 1885, a 33-year-old woman, Karoline, was admitted to Sct. Hans Hospital. She was convinced that she was pregnant and she said that the child's father was a well known priest living in Copenhagen.

She remained in the hospital for the next 50 years – the rest of her life – and painted some beautiful paintings, made patchwork and paper-work. She wrote about herself: 'I am the Virgin Mary, Magdalene Ebbesen.' Her ideas, as she expressed them in words, were recorded as was her visual world, illustrated in her pictures. She was intensively preoccupied with themes of birth and death. In 1985 a book was written about Karoline (Reisby and Skogemann 1985). The book is illustrated with her pictures. Through the years, doctors and nurses in the hospital had taken care of these expressions of her inner world. Today you can see Karoline's pictures in the hospital museum. Nobody, however, seemed to use her pictures as a way of trying to understand and help her.

A hundred years passed from the day Karoline was admitted to Sct. Hans Hospital. In 1985 a 35-year-old man was referred for a psychological examination at the same hospital. He came to the very house in which Karoline had spent so many years. We will call him Paul. In the Rorschach-test he showed us a glimpse of his imaginary world, which he was able to express in spite of his great anxiety and severe personality disturbances.

In the year he was admitted, he wrote a letter to the staff in the ward telling them about the significance of his artistic expressions: 'I draw using the colours without thinking what to make. Often figures come out of it. They show my ideas, those with more anxiety or less psychotic fantasies, but also those about feeling safe and having good feelings. When my ideas become figures on paper outside myself, I can look upon them more objectively, perhaps like other people would look upon them, and in this way they are no longer the whole reality. It becomes antipsychotic and a way to limit my anxiety.' So far as we know, he did not then show any of his drawings to anyone.

He had been in psychotherapy for three years with the first author of this chapter (M) when this chapter was written. The second author was the supervisor. We hope, in this chapter, to illustrate aspects of a psychotherapeutic process with a man who created his illustrated world around the fairy-tale figure Pinocchio and who was able to grow through his identification with a small wooden doll.

Pinocchio is the main figure in an Italian fairy tale written in 1883 by Carlo Lorenzini (Collodi 1920). He is a marionette made of wood. The story starts with a carpenter finding a magic piece of wood. He gives it to his old friend Gepetto who makes a marionette out of it. The magic wood becomes a living doll, changing in the end to a real living boy.

The story can be looked upon as a psychodrama in which the growth of a boy is followed through seven developmental stages. When he meets challenges, he will often regress and behave as a very small boy who does not want to learn anything and will not take any responsibility (Brun and Skovgaard 1983). There are several animals around Pinocchio, and a fairy. These all take part in his life and have a symbolic significance representing drives, and manifestations of the conscience. At the end of the story, Pinocchio shows great courage when he rescues his old father; at this stage he becomes a real flesh and blood boy (see Roheim 1985).

An Extension of Paul's Story

Paul was very isolated and lonely as a child. He was afraid of other children. According to what he has said, his mother did not like boys. He should have been a girl, but by mistake he became a boy. His grandmother said that he was born with a tail and black hair, which fell off. It took a long time before he was born. He was stuck, 'It hurt my mother, the boy was too big. He did not want to be born. It took many hours.' Paul was unhappy at school and was referred to the school psychologist.

When he was 17, he started to hear voices, felt anxious, and developed paranoid ideas. He had a great need to regress to babyhood. Sometimes, he would wrap himself up in sheets and would lie in a chair, wetting his nappies and sucking his fingers. Later, he would suck his dummy, which he would hide carefully from his parents. He has kept his dummy ever since.

Paul finished school and began higher education, but it was hard for him to concentrate. In his early twenties he was granted a pension, based on his mental illness. Paul dated girls now and then, never being able to establish a mature relationship. He was often hospitalized in psychiatric hospitals. During the period in which he was in individual psychotherapy he was gradually hospitalized less frequently, and only for short periods. He has never been treated with psychoactive drugs for more than short periods, because he has been very much against it.

Paul and His Pictures – The First Year in Psychotherapy

During his first session, in May 1986, Paul sucked his fingers and crawled on the floor, trying to cut himself with a pair of scissors he had taken with him. He used a very private language, and thus it was difficult to understand him. He was confused as to whether his therapist had changed identity and was actually one of his former therapists. He wet his pants, and continued doing so for a long period. It seemed difficult for him to sit on a chair and talk to his therapist, so she chose to put out colours and a notebook. She told him that he could use these if he felt like it, and she would take a few notes while talking with him. In this way both were preoccupied and the meeting was less frightening to him. He was satisfied that his therapist was taking notes and said: 'You take care of me.'

The idea of letting Paul paint during his sessions came up as a way to provide structure and space, while also establishing a relationship which was less frightening for him. The painting process was his own, but it also provided access to talking. Talking about his paintings is talking about Paul. It is a way for M to get into contact with his feelings: indirectly, through a better intuitive understanding of what is going on; directly, when responding to his work. The pictures present something stable; they are always there, and they give continuity to his life. Simultaneously, they help him to keep a necessary distance between him and his inner world; between him, his therapist and his inner world; and between him, his therapist and wider aspects of the outer world, which is expressed so clearly: ' When my ideas become figures on paper outside myself, I can look upon them more objectively.' His first drawing is shown as Figure 6.1.

He made this drawing without any comments. The title **Indefrysning** illustrates a private world of his, meaning something like 'icebound' or 'freezing up.' The big figure makes associations with a womb. He has presented similar figures often since then. To Paul, black often seems to show something threatening or frightening. It may signify anger in him and anger projected onto the outer world, whereas green seems to symbolize hope and good feelings. He has said that red has been his favourite colour; it is the child's colour, he says. He often uses it in situations in which he describes himself as small and frightened. Arrows and triangles are frequent elements in his drawings. They may represent phallic aspects. They also seem to illustrate destructive forces, something threatening in himself and in the outer world.

One day M feels insecure about his mood, so she says 'Paint the two of us in the office.' In this way she focuses on their mutual relationship without getting too close or being private.

Paul says while drawing: 'I will be OK, don't you think so? It is you I am painting; you are inside an orange sleeping bag,' and he continues 'Have you got sixteen children?' The atmosphere in the picture is peaceful and the colours warm.

Figure 6.1

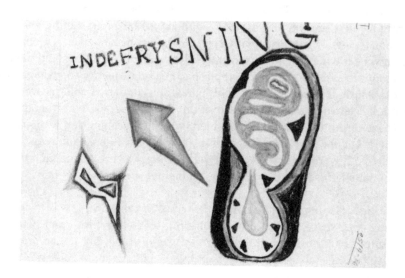

Figure 6.2

Being in a sleeping bag might symbolize being in a womb. Paul also seems to think of M as a mother capable of coping with sixteen children. The picture may indicate the experience of unclear generational boundaries, lack of differentiation, symbiosis. M is an unborn baby and a mother at the same time. Paul may also have the fantasy that he is one of sixteen babies inside her. No further associations or interpretations came up. The painting gave the impression that he was feeling at ease on that particular day.

Often his session started with his returning to the last session's drawings. During periods in which he has been very sick, it has been possible to go back to the old days and see how he was able to continue life at that stage. He often talks about himself using the word 'he' instead of 'I.' He explains it quite clearly. 'It is easier to talk about him than to talk about me.'

Paul and Pinocchio

One day, after a year had passed, Paul came in. He was feeling miserable; he said he had lost his *Pinocchio* book. It turned out later that he had lost it as a child, not just recently, as one might have expected. The experience of time is often disturbed in sensitive people.

That day he was very upset. He said that a woman he knew had bitten him and beaten him; he expressed the desire to kill her. Gradually, he turned his anger towards M. He took the black paint and threw it on the floor; it cracked, and he shouted that M was a fascist like all the others, 'and they shall all die, and he will die as well.' He seemed very angry and was very threatening.

> M: Sit down and don't make such a noise – won't you need the black colour any longer?
>
> Paul: Yes.
>
> M: Shouldn't you find it again then?.
>
> *Paul takes it from the floor.*

At the end of this session M asks if Paul wanted to frighten her. He said that if she had become frightened, he would not have been able to use her and then she could not help him. When he left that day, he took her hand and said 'It is good you are looking after me, telling me what is right and wrong. It is good that you are strong.'

The black paint that was thrown on the floor seems to be closely connected with his anger. When M asks him if he won't need it again, she tries to make him understand that she knows the angry feelings are there, and that they will be able to cope with them. She also tries to show Paul a way in which he may gradually get in touch with his anger and sorrow, leading his attention to a concrete object, the black paint on the floor. The black colour is a tool to express his feelings in acceptable ways. This day in May was the beginning of a long period during which Pinocchio was an essential figure in the sessions.

Two months later, Paul talked about how he used to beat his smaller brother as a child, and he asked M to bring some more black paint. Some weeks later M noticed that Paul had put a new block of black paint in the box and taken away the cracked one in such a discreet way that she had not noticed when it happened. Paul's first illustration of Pinocchio is seen in Figure 6.3.

Figure 6.3

Commenting on his first picture, Paul says: 'He was in the land of milk and honey. He always lied because they did something he must not do. He got donkey ears because he broke things and ate layer cakes, but not when Gepetto saw it. He is four years old and will remain so. He was made of wood, and he danced in a clumsy way, and went to the circus, where Yvonne was (Yvonne is an imaginary friend from Paul's childhood; she is not in the story), and they came to the land of milk and honey. But he is clumsy and made of wood sometimes, but his ears are donkey ears. Then they broke all the furniture, and the ugly boy showed them how to do it, pile up layer cakes, break windows, chairs, and eat more layer cakes.' Paul becomes very excited, paints the red heart and is absorbed in sucking his finger. While drawing, he develops fantasies about urinating with a girl and being punished by his mother.

We wondered why Pinocchio meant so much to Paul. Pinocchio goes through a developmental process, for a long time being a pre-school child, a very small impulse-ridden boy. In the end, he becomes a real living boy, no longer made of wood. He has then grown and changed far beyond the stage which Paul had reached emotionally. However, Paul provided part of the explanation very soon, saying to M: 'Pinocchio is four years and will never become any older.' Several times he repeats that M must never read any further than to 'the land of milk and honey.' Otherwise, the story will become sad, frightening and macabre, 'something with a dark tunnel, where children are caught and thrown together.' During the first year of working with *Pinocchio*, the theme of birth often turns up in his drawings, and the impossible process of becoming a grown-up person.

In supervision we discuss what kind of *Pinocchio* book Paul knows, and it appears that he only knows the Walt Disney version of the fairy tale. M tells him that the story really comes from an old Italian fairy tale.

Soon after, he puts a note on the table. On it he has written the author's name and the number of the book in the library, referring to the real story. When asked about the note Paul says that he would like to meet the 'real' Pinocchio, but he will not borrow the book himself. M suggests to him that they read the book, and he agrees. During the following period when he comes for his session M has prepared a small piece from the story, which she either tells him or reads to him. However, it is always up to Paul to decide whether they read anything on that particular day, if it is time to stop, or if it is a good idea to return to something which has already been read. At certain stages in the very dramatic story, she moderated the language.

In June 1988, Paul draws a picture of Pinocchio and his birth (see Figures 6.4 and 6.5), and he says: 'Birth – it has to be slow like the birth of Paul, who did not want to be born.' Commenting on these pictures, he says of Figure 6.4 'Pinocchio is locked up'. Of the next drawing (Figure 6.5) he says: 'Pinocchio is in the tree. He may stay there a bit longer, for he is not going to be born yet.' Paul talks about his own birth, the wish not to be born, and his wishes to be a girl and he fantasizes around this theme. He says: 'If Pinocchio pulls Gepetto by his hair, do you then think Gepetto would get so angry that he would throw Pinocchio into the compost heap?' In September he draws 'Pinocchio in bed.' The fairy has put Pinocchio to bed (Figure 6.6).

The figure on the right illustrates his anxiety, and the one on the left shows more courage in relation to getting out of bed and into the world. He says: 'The white one snuggles down and is afraid. The coloured one wants to break frames and play.' The picture has associations with a very early foetal stage in development. It shows the conflict between wishing to regress and wishing to grow.

Next time he talks about the fascists. Paul says: 'It is important that you don't become so afraid of fascists that you become a fascist yourself.' He says to M that she should not be too worried about him, because it is important to use energy during the sessions in a good way. The following stage in his drawings shows Pinocchio out of bed. Paul asks M if she thinks Pinocchio can be strong enough to get out and survive in the real world. 'In this story the fairy is not just a stream of light. She is a human being, who wants to become his sister and she belongs to reality, not just a beam of light in your imagination. She has real hands and she can make something.' In a very poetic way he talks indirectly about the psychotherapeutic alliance.

Figure 6.4

Figure 6.5

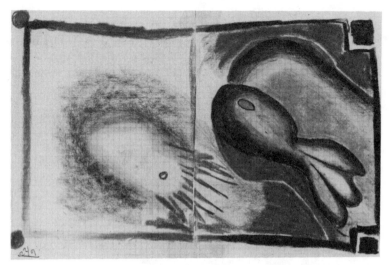

Figure 6.6

Some weeks later he is worried: 'They [members of the staff] say that he has been coming for several years [referring to psychotherapy, which has lasted for two years then]'. Paul thinks this is cheating, because he has only been coming a few days, if the hours are counted. He is afraid that he will lose his therapist if she leaves the hospital. M says that she knows he needs to come for a long time.

They talk about Pinocchio, the difficulties in working with him. Perhaps the story goes too fast, and M asks if it would be a good idea to stop the story for a while. Paul says: 'We must not stop, but we will have to return to earlier parts of the story. It is necessary to stay and put Pinocchio to bed again. He will have to be a small boy for some time, but they must not stop too long and consider things for too long, because then it will be too late.' In this way Paul seems to express some very important aspects of timing during psychotherapy.

He then tries to compare himself with a house attacked by sponges. It is tempting to pull it down, but it can be repaired.

In November 1988 he gives M a picture which he has made at home. He says that now and then she will have something which has been finished (see Figure 6.7). His comments are 'crumbled.' 'The fox and the cat have left him all alone under the tree, but then the blue fairy came and helped him.' The dummy, the blue tears and the blue hand may be seen in the picture with the broken Pinocchio. Paul has expressed fantasies about a foetus that has disintegrated. He has related these fantasies to his younger brother, whom he had fantasies to kill when he was a boy.

After this period Paul starts gradually to separate himself from Pinocchio. They become two different persons. He explains very clearly that it is easier to work with problems when they belong to Pinocchio than to work with his own problems, but he knows quite well whom they are talking about. He starts expressing thoughts concerning his chances 'of becoming so strong that he will be able to survive in the real world in reality,' and for the first time he gives the impression that he thinks that, maybe, he will be able to succeed. However, help from the fairy is needed; but gradually also Gepetto becomes significant.

Figure 6.7

Apparently Paul had always had a poor relationship with his father. He has described him as disgusting, and this is how he experiences Gepetto at the beginning. He projects his own feelings about his father into the figure Gepetto. As the reading of the story progresses, Gepetto acquires a greater and more positive significance for Paul. Paul can now express his wish to 'find' Gepetto the father and get on good terms with him.

In the autumn of 1988 he makes Figure 6.8. 'Pinocchio, who has now come out into the garden.' He wonders whether it will be necessary to take away the wild animals (on the left side) or perhaps they will become like those on the right side, which are not so dangerous. He touches M's hand very gently, and she puts both of her hands around Pinocchio. Now he is protected. A little later Paul objects; M cannot sit like that for ever and what then? M takes a piece of paper, tears a hole in the middle and puts it over (see Figure 6.9). They talk about

Figure 6.8

the protective significance; M takes another piece of paper and makes a bigger hole, so that a bit of the wild animals can be seen. She puts it over the picture instead of the first one (Figure 6.10). Paul objects to this; the hole is too big, and he puts the one with the small hole back again. He says: 'The fairy is going here,' and he starts to paint the fairy. The colour of her frock is exactly the same as M's sweater. He looks carefully when comparing the colours.

He says: 'Perhaps the fairy could make him so well that he can live outside the house, even if there were wild animals. This would require that he remembered what he wanted to forget, that he should know it was true that it had happened. Then he would become very unhappy, so maybe he does not want to know it.' He starts to paint Gepetto, but does not finish him that day.

We do not really know what Paul had to forget. It seems to have to do with very traumatic experiences as a small boy, the feeling that he was never accepted by his mother, either as a child or as a boy. During the same period in which Paul becomes more clearly differentiated from Pinocchio, he begins to talk more directly to M. He uses her name, and he does not need to talk about himself in the third person so often any longer. He is also able to tolerate M's using his name now and then, when talking to him. He comments on this process as follows: 'Reality becomes more and more clear, but it is dirty as a rat, and things are double, and you must see reality to be able to live in it.' Seeing things double may refer to painful ambivalent feelings.

He expresses his feeling that he is not quite sure whether he wants to become absolutely well. 'Maybe it is enough to see more things in a more relaxed way – be less frightened and thus get more out of his life. Just so that you can walk among others without being so frightened and "shrunk". Feel the pleasure in

Figure 6.9

Figure 6.10

believing that of course there are fascists in the world, and people who are silly and mean, but it is not entirely like that, and not all are like that.'

He starts talking about his early memories and fantasies about his parents and their relationship and sex life, as he experienced it from his bed in his parents' bedroom. 'It was some stranger who had come in, and it would be impolite to tell them to leave, even if it was disgusting.' It is hard for Paul to talk about these matters and particularly about his father, but he insists on doing so, 'for you cannot always walk around thinking other people are disgusting, even if you get frightened, when it "touches too close" – it is as if named flesh was touched, but we have to talk about it, little by little. For Pinocchio is able to tolerate what happens now, because he is able to remember something, which happened before and he can use it.'

Paul now hears about Pinocchio, who is going to attend school and work hard, be responsible. All these demands make Paul feel tense and cross. He explains to M that perhaps Pinocchio does not want to be a living boy all the time, only now and then. Paul draws the fairy/witch and Pinocchio and says that she is mother and now she is also the fairy, the witch, the angel and the sister. Gradually, he is able to tolerate more. He explains that 'never before has he felt that there could be a little witch in a person without it mattering very much or without it becoming dangerous for that reason. Probably there is a small witch and demanding part in everyone even in the fairy.' (See Figure 6.11.)

He ends by saying 'it is probably important to learn to tell, even if one is not able to, when you know that certain things are impossible, even if you try very hard.' Then he draws a big ear on the fairy to make her hear what he says. Before he leaves, he comes up with a request, which he has never done before. He asks M to change the time for his weekly session to make it fit better with his train.

In the following months Paul is preoccupied with the process of integrating good and evil. He tries to understand that people in the world are not necessarily

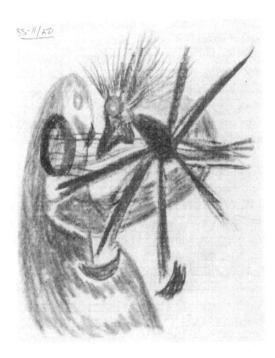

Figure 6.11

either white or black. He begins to realize that he is able to influence his surroundings and thus get more control into his life.

In the spring of 1989 Paul's movements are better coordinated. He sometimes laughs as if feeling released during his sessions. He is able to laugh at others but also at himself. He is dressed in better and cleaner clothes. He has cut his long hair and washes it more regularly. Often when his hair was cut before, he became acutely psychotic, but he is no longer afraid of having it cut. He is pleased 'not to look like someone you feel like pricking with an umbrella.' He is not so often wet now. One day he suddenly asks for the toilet. He then goes to the toilet, when he would otherwise wet himself.

He has started clearing his flat saying: 'If it is going to stop being all untidy and "creased" inside you, it is necessary that what is untidy and messy around you disappears.' With M he plans what he will do before they meet again, and nearly always he has done a little more. He has done something on his own, and it seems very important for him to prove his capacity and independence in this way.

From an Animal to a Marionette and Further Development

In schizophrenic persons' artistic expressions one often meets fantasies concerning contaminated creatures, half animals half human beings. This was the case in Karoline's imaginary world and in Paul's. In psychoanalytic terms one would refer to manifestations of primary process thinking. In mythology and religions from all over the world in all times we likewise find manifestations of contamination. In the Christian tradition, we think of fresco paintings from the eleventh century illustrating the devil, who has horns, horse's hooves and a tail, as if he were partly an animal.

Paul's fantasies about being an animal were expressed very early in psychotherapy. He said: 'As a child I was an animal. The fur had been taken off, and they tried to make him believe that they were his parents. He should believe that he was a human being, otherwise he was in a box. It was sitting looking at slides, and then they gave him something' (see Figure 6.12, 'blue lips'). This reminds us of his grandmother telling him that he was born with a tail. Whether she has actually said so, or whether it is Paul's fantasy, we do not know, of course, but he never felt that he was loved as a child, either by his parents, or by his grandparents. Paul's fantasies in childhood included two girls, Pauline and Yvonne. He would often feel that he was one of these girls. Many of his pictures have an androgynous quality; human beings or parts of bodies with female as well as male sexual organs show us aspects of his personality development, but also his developmental arrest.

All this came up in the sessions before Pinocchio entered the stage. Pinocchio is a boy, but he is made of wood. His name means pine kernel – something alive, which can also grow. When Pinocchio lies and behaves in an irresponsible way he changes and becomes almost like an animal with donkey ears.

Figure 6.12

Paul has stressed several times that Pinocchio is four years old, exactly the age Paul was when he got a younger sister and started wetting himself again like a baby. At first he would not face the end of the story when Pinocchio grows up and becomes a real living boy. He refused to accept the end of the story as part of it. This illustrates quite clearly that it has been difficult for him to reach school age and thus a mature developmental stage in childhood, the latency period.

Reading *Pinocchio* to Paul takes time, but Paul now seems to see perspectives in Pinocchio's life. Perhaps he will be able to follow Pinocchio a long way yet and survive in the real world.

Theoretical Considerations
It has been stated in psychoanalytic literature that the borderline personality emerges when the mother has been adequate only up to the holding phase of separation individuation (Grotstein, 1982). As a result of her subsequent inadequacy, the child never completes the transition from symbiosis to separation and individuation.

We know that Paul's mother was in psychiatric hospitals for long periods during his childhood. He has illustrated fantasies of being a broken foetus not wanting to be born and suffering because 'it hurt my mother'. He did not separate his own pain from his mother's pain and perhaps his development was disturbed from the very beginning of life, even before he was born.

The symbiotic wishes as they were illustrated in psychotherapy have been very strong (sucking his fingers, carrying a dummy, wetting himself). These wishes are clearly illustrated in his pictures which did, at the same time, seem to help him keep control. Separated aspects of the self were projected onto the image of external objects 'the fascists', and for long periods he felt persecuted. He lived a very isolated and lonely life. Gradually, he has been able to realize that perhaps there is a little witch even in the fairy.

In his article 'Helplessness in the Helpers' Adler (1982) has described severely psychotic patients as not being able to maintain an internal image of a basically helpful person without it being overwhelmed or lost because of negative introjects or feelings. These patients have intense feelings of loss and abandonment. They never had 'good enough' mothers who were not afraid of their own or their child's anger. It is well known that these patients are very difficult to work with. For the therapist the transference/counter transference situation is complicated, as Adler points out. Clarification, interpretation and confrontation must be administered with great skill and sensitivity.

In this process it is extremely important that the patients discover they cannot destroy the therapist. Paul explained it when he said that if his therapist had become frightened, he would not be able to use her.

As it has been pointed out by Wallerstein (1989) real treatments in actual practice within the psychoanalytic frame of reference are often intermingled blends of expressive, interpretive and supportive stabilizing elements. This has also been the case in the treatment of Paul. The psychotherapeutic technique applying tools such as pictures, toys and fairy tales are well known within psychoanalytically oriented child psychotherapy. We have found this play therapy, as one might call it, a great help in our work with severely disturbed adult patients.

CHAPTER 7

The Language of Symbols in Fairy Tales
Illustrative Examples

Birgitte Brun

The idea of the collective unconscious seen as part of the psyche, which fundamentally unites people, with no national or racial borders was developed by C.G. Jung. The archetypal images have their origin in the collective unconscious; Nyborg mentions as an example of an archetypal image the divine child, which has been described in the chapter on Peter Pan (Nyborg 1962).

As already said, the archetypes of the collective unconscious are intrinsically formless psychic structures, which become visible in art. An archetype may manifest itself in different ways, depending upon culture and individuality. As expressed by van Eenwyk (1991) 'Archetypes break up the linear flow of consciousness infusing it with a chaotic/non-linear flow'. He also expresses the thoughts that 'only by becoming strong enough to dwell on the boundary, where chaos and recapitulation of conflict preside, can the analyst keep the opposing forces at a manageable level.'

Focusing your attention on the chaotic/non-linear flow, it feels natural at the same time to think of symbols in fairy tales as polyvalent, as explained by Holbek (1987), and it is important to apply a gestalt-psychological approach. Using fairy tales in psychotherapy, this approach should include not only the story in which you find the symbol, but also the patient's story and inner world as we have already discussed it.

In a psychotherapeutic hour a patient may call your attention to the tree in *Cinderella*, which could have a positive potential symbolic value. However, if the patient refers specifically to the 'Cinderella tree', you should not forget that in *Cinderella*, you are also confronted with serious bodily harm and blood-shedding. It is not enough to notice the green colour, if red is right behind it, perhaps telling you about the patient's fight with destructive fantasies and impulses.

When interpreting fairy tale symbols within a psychotherapeutic frame of reference, it is sometimes difficult to see the gestalt, which also includes the patient's inner world, and if you have seen it to stay with it. If the therapist closes his eyes, not being able to face and feel a frightening gestalt, how then should he be able to help the patient? These were my reflections, when I had failed to focus my attention on the red behind the green (in the patient's preoccupation with the *Cinderella* tree). The tree was there, clear and calm, but this was not all. As I looked upon it later, I had overlooked an unconscious signal of warning from the patient, and perhaps also a cry for help.

The selected symbols have been interpreted according to the fairy tale literature. In some cases they are also seen in a psychotherapeutic perspective. In relation to fairy tales I have found it helpful to work with three groups of symbols.

1. **Symbols of Nature** such as the wood, the sea, human beings, animals, plants and so forth.

2. **Magical/Mythological Symbols** such as mermaids, pixies, trolls, angels.

3. **Culturally Created Symbols** such as the key, the doll, gold, the spinning-wheel, hats, magic objects and human beings, where the cultural aspect is emphasized such as kings, queens, princes, tailors, gardeners etc.

If you refer to a symbol as belonging to one of these three groups, you look upon the symbol in itself and not at the significance of the symbol. To decide which group a symbol belongs to is a fairly simple task, whereas the interpretative process could be complicated and multi-faceted.

The oldest symbols are probably symbols of nature and the youngest symbols the culturally created symbols. According to McCully (1971) one of the earliest psychological tasks for man was to acquire freedom from bondage to the laws of instinct that applied to all animal forms of life. As for the religious/mythological symbols, McCully emphasizes that the ancient Greeks used the word *mythos* to mean a container for essentials of truth, and very important in relation to man's development.

When a symbol has been defined as belonging to one of the three groups, the next thing to do will be to look for its significance, that is, to try to find an interpretation which is natural in relation to the context in which the symbol is seen. When looking upon selected symbols and their possible significance, we sometimes relate them to the inner world of people we have got to know through psychotherapy. This is also a way to illustrate associative work essential for the psychotherapist. The interpretation of the different symbols has been taken from the literature which has been included in this book.

Symbols of Nature

The Animals often represent the instincts. The lion symbolizes power and sensuality.

Animal Body an externalization of an inferior position. The change from animal to human being could then indicate entering the position of the grown up person. Helpers in the body of animals or the ability to change into an animal could illustrate sexual maturity, since the animals symbolize the body.

A female psychotic patient described how she felt that her hands were changing into claws. In such a situation it may be helpful for the psychotherapist to think of the frequent theme of change from human being to animal as we meet it in fairy tales and mythology. It may help him understand the patient, even if he does not choose to mention fairy tales at all.

Artemis, the famous huntress in Greek mythology, is often transformed into a deer. The hunter and hunted are secretly identical. It is essential to think of this in psychotherapy. What a person fears most of all is sometimes also what he is longing for. A young woman avoiding contact with men, fearing that they will be sexually threatening, may indicate that on an unconscious level she fears her own sexuality. She is afraid to lose control. Sometimes we as therapists focus our attention on the deer, and are blind to Artemis behind.

The Bear in fairy tales could be a magically changed prince.

The Bird – in mythology the dead soul may be seen as a bird. The bird may also symbolize the very beginning of life. In this way the symbol of the bird may contain the birth motif and also the death motif, as illustrated in *Peter Pan.* When the bird motif turns up in psychotherapy, it is important to bear in mind the theme of birth and the theme of death.

A young male patient had been difficult to make contact with on anything more than a very superficial level. In the hospital ward where he lived an old man became seriously ill, and after some days he died. The young man had sat at his bedside talking to him, holding his hand, and he had been very helpful. When later he talked about the old man dying he said: 'You are never as lonely in your life as when you are born and when you are dying.' He seemed to touch on existential matters and also his personal story, since apparently he had been let down at a very early stage in life, and as a very young man had been involved in destructive fights.

Blood – when magic objects are touched by blood, the blood cannot be washed off them. The motif of blood that cannot be washed off is an ancient theme. It could be a sign that some evil deed – usually murder – was committed. Blood may also be related to the first intercourse when the hymen is broken. Defloration is an irreversible event, cannot be washed off.

A young male patient who had killed a person was talking about his future life. He could see no future for himself, since his serious act would always be there. Suddenly he got up, and went to get a cup of water to drink. Soon after he was washing the cup and the way in which he was drying it made one think of the blood that cannot be washed off. His unconscious message seemed much stronger than his words.

The Death of an Archetypal Figure is its depersonification, for archetypes cannot die. They are internal, instinctive, inherited dispositions. If they lose their human shape it means they are not functioning any more in a form which can easily be integrated into human life.

The Dog is usually positive in its relation to man – a friend, a guardian, but as the carrier of madness also much dreaded. In earlier times it was thought to bring disease and pestilence.

Earth and Water going into the earth or the water in a dream may be a descent into the unconscious, but if there are layers and traces of former civilizations, it would indicate that there were elements which had once been conscious. The struggle of the adolescent male always carries the danger of death as, for instance, the trial of the young man through water and fire in various myths.

Feathers representing thoughts and fantasies and may take the place of the bird (*pars pro toto*).

Flowers are symbols of wholeness. Flower opening represents the opening of eternal life.

The Frog is an amphibian (*ampho* means both, *bios* means life). It is an animal with two types of life, fishlike as a tadpole and predominantly land-bound as a frog. It is therefore an excellent symbol of the metamorphosis from one world to another. It is the messenger from the sphere of the more fluid psychic world to the solid, material world.

The Hair – spiritual requirements. Hair symbolizes life. Power and strength is in the hair. Bearing this in mind it may become easier to understand why psychotic children and schizophrenic adults may sometimes get into a panic if you cut their hair.

The Heart contains the soul. The soul is a fire in the hearth of the heart. Sickness of heart is sickness of the soul and of the body's vital energy.

The Island is a magic realm inhabited by otherworldly figures. Islands often harbour projections of the unconscious psychic sphere. Islands of the dead. Never Neverland in *Peter Pan* is an island.

The Moon. The moon's name and image have become those of goddess, queen of Heaven and mother in the imagination of men. The attributes of the moon in primitive thought are transformed characters, functions and actions of primitive woman, which are regarded as being divided and controlled by the magic power of the moon. The moon image is related in man's imagination to the lives of women and burdened with the obscure mingled feelings they excite.

Mountain – Mother Earth. A place of orientation, a symbol of self knowledge that leads to inspired wisdom. A patient expressed a period in psychotherapy as very difficult, like trying to climb a huge mountain. She was afraid of getting into contact with unconscious feelings having to do with her relationship with her mother, so it seemed.

Plants getting nourishment from the earth correspond to the body's life, a close connection with the unconscious. As part of midlife development men sometimes have an increasing interest in nurturing functions such as growing a garden, which may at the same time symbolize a change in the investment of energy to become more concerned about inner values.

Poison being offered might appear as certain highly destructive thoughts and feelings, which one should forcefully reject. In the case of the hero, he is tempted to remain infantile.

The Raven is said to symbolize the devil or, in alchemy, the dark Mercurius (his black soul challenges the instinct of self preservation). The raven could be clever, good or bad.

Rose is a symbol of the self.

Salt in the sea, a bitterness also associated with tears and with sadness 'the salt of wisdom'.

Wanderers are a symbol of longing, the restless urge which never finds its object of nostalgia for the lost mother. The impetus for the hero is the need to break free from the mother, and his wandering is an oscillating path between a desire for recognition of and connectedness to the mother and the wish to be independent of her.

The Wind is well known as a symbol of the inspiring spiritual quality of the unconscious. This motif would mean that imagination and thoughts are wandering. A too rational, ordered organized attitude means loss of contact with the feminine element.

Woods – in the middle of the woods, extremely important events take place. Prince Ring chases in the woods, that is unconsciousness. He loses his way in the fog, where his ability to see is reduced. In psychotherapy you sometimes have to venture to go into the woods in spite of the fear of getting lost.

Magical/Mythological Symbols

Dragons symbolize deep unconscious layers.

Granny Evergreen – timelessness, something eternal transcending time, since everything in nature fades and dies.

Giants are characterized by their size. In folk belief thunder is thought to be giants bowling or hammering. Erratic stone formations are composed of stones tossed by giants in play, and fog appears when the giantesses hang up their washing. In the *Edda* the giant has a sword, which separates fire and ice (the opposite poles). Giants are only half human, they show strength and stupidity, they are easy to deceive. They may go berserk.

Fairies – friendliness, courtesy, beauty, understanding (the thirteenth evil fairy, a woman of wisdom like the paradisiacal serpent). The mother giving good things (twelve good fairies), and then in a twinkling destroying all the values (the evil fairy). In the end restoration and balance is created.

Mermaids – communication between aquatic and earthly existence. When the wicked angels fell down from the sky, some landed in woods, others in houses and farms, and others in gardens and lakes. From the first ones came elves, from the second pixies and creatures living under the earth and from the last ones mermaids.

From Karoline, a schizophrenic woman and an artist who has lived at Sct. Hans Hospital for 50 years, we learned 'The angel is a small dwarf'. Presents from dwarfs can be interpreted as inner qualities in the girl (externalization).

Queen Juliane Marie, the mother of the Danish King Frederik VIII, characterized herself in the following way: 'I have an angel's face, the body of a toad and a devil's mind'.

The Mother Principle is primarily on the side of nature in the sense of the instincts, the physical drives, as a force for change and the renewal of life. The mother figure in her destructive guise as shaper of destiny,

Trolls are beings combining human with nonhuman characteristics. Trolls may express that something primitive in man is in control.

The Witch will often illustrate the negative mother image.The witch is often seen as a tempting creature trying to persuade the hero to do wicked things. Through this we have an opportunity to increase our consciousness through identification with the hero. If we could see our greed, envy, wickedness, malice and hate, then we could use both sides positively, because they have so much life. The witch gives tasks, which the heroine solves by means of a helper often taking the shape of an animal. Witches may go out at night as fox souls.

Cultural Symbols

Baldness – old age, masculinity.

Ball – symbol of the self.

A Coffin – a picture of a stage, in which you have no connection with life.

Doll – representing the deepest essence of the mother figure, though not the human side. Dolls will often serve as transitional objects in the small girl's life, and the doll motif related to fairy tales or dreams during psychotherapy would make you think of the very early relationship with the mother.

The Fisherman is on the threshold between the solid earth and fluctuating liquid world. The treasures he tries to catch are evanescent like our dreams, which so easily evaporate in the daytime.

The Forbidden Room with its frightful secret. A complex repressed, could have to do with body-image and sexual curiosity in the child. It has to do with something frightening, but is also fascinating.

The Gardener is led to his occupation by his ability to further the growth of all that is good.

The Girl in the Well – she meets witches etc. The child leaves home, but she returns to her parents again; the sexual and social aspects are not yet quite developed.

Gold – spiritual rather than material treasure. Gold may symbolize sexual maturity.

Goldsmith – power and intuitive sight.

The Key that opens the door to a secret room suggests associations with the male sexual organ, particularly in first intercourse when the hymen is broken and blood gets on it. Defloration is an irreversible event, cannot be washed off.

The key also gives access to the unconscious, to important values and to insight. We have emphasized the wish to know more in the young woman who said 'She has got the key to the truth' (referring to a piece of jewelry shaped like a key). This young woman expressed the idea that she had given birth to eight children, and that she was three years old when she had her first child. As I saw it, she had never had time to be a child, since she 'was a mother' by the age of three and associating this with the symbol of the key, you could not help wondering whether she had been a sexually abused child.

Kitchen – analogous to the stomach, the centre of emotion, relationship with the mother.

The Mirror – the very young woman was not allowed to look in the mirror in olden days, neither was the pregnant woman, nor the woman who had just given birth nor sick people. This could be dangerous (magic thinking). In China, people have carried a mirror on their backs as a protection. The protection is seen in the recognition of what is coming from behind, namely the unconscious. Schizophrenic people sometimes look in the mirror and express the frightening idea that they are changing. Violent and anxiety-provoking thoughts and feelings, experiences of being possessed by evil powers are reflected when the person looks in the mirror.

The Ring – symbol of the self, especially as a factor that creates relatedness. It means the completion of the inner essential being.

The Robber – selfish, seeks to appropriate all the material goods and sensory pleasures of his world.

The Shoe – symbol of the vagina. In *Cinderella*, when the slipper fits, the soul, the anima is ready for the marriage with the prince. Real growth reflects itself in all phases and aspects of an individual's activity, sublime and modest, and encompass along with the intellectual and emotional also the instinctual and the vegetative functions, as described by Vibeke Arndal (1985).

The Spinning Wheel and spinning. A type of reasoning which is detached from active life. In *Sleeping Beauty* it is high up in the castle's tower, in a little cubbyhole behind a little door, which can be opened with a rusty key. It is in the head, where we spin the intellectual threads which are deadening our feelings and deep beliefs, especially if the mental processes are shut off from the rest of our soul for such a long time that the key to the door (between heart and brain) has become rusty.

There is the spinning wheel of the beautiful virgin of the Northland sitting on a rainbow and spinning silver and gold dresses that will clothe her, the anima, when she is ready to descend and unite herself with the ideal male, the animus. A maturational process is illustrated.

Spinning can also be live thoughts which render the soul richer. This is one of the many examples of the polyvalent significance of symbols in fairy tales.

The Stepmother – with one hand she destroys, with the other she leads to fulfilment. The symbol of the unconscious in its destructive role. May illustrate the development of the young girl, who sees all the negative qualities in her mother when she reaches puberty. In this way you could look upon the stepmother as belonging to a certain stage in the young woman's personality development.

Bibliography

Adler, G. (1982) Helplessness in the Helper. In P.L. Giovacchini and L.B. Boyer (eds.) *Technical Factors in the Treatment of the Severely Disturbed Patient*. New York: Jason Aronson. pp.385–408.

Allport, G.W. (1967) *The Individual and His Religion*. New York: MacMillan.

Andersen, H.C. (1966) *Fairy Tales, vol.1*. Odense: Flensted.

Andersen, H.C. (1966) *Fairy Tales, vol.2*. Odense: Flensted.

Andersen, H.C. (1966) *Fairy Tales, vol.4*. Odense: Flensted.

Andersen, H.C. (1979) *Tommelise*, 2nd ed. (Drawings by Elsa Beskow.) Copenhagen: Gyldendal.

Arndal, V. (1985) *Heksen i håret*. Copenhagen: Lindhardt og Ringhof.

Asper, K. (1989) *Ravnen i Glasbjerget*. Copenhagen: Gyldendal. (Translated from German.)

Bannerman, H. (1900) *Little Black Sambo*. Philadelphia: Frederick A. Stokes.

Barrie, J.M. (1902) *The Little White Bird*. London: Hodder and Stoughton.

Barrie, J.M. (1911) *Peter Pan and Wendy*. London: Hodder and Stoughton.

Barrie, J.M. (1924) *Mary Rose*. London: Hodder and Stoughton.

Bettelheim, B. (1976) *The Uses of Enchantment: The Meaning and Importance of Fairy Tales*. London: Penguin Books.

Birkhäuser-Oeri, S., and von Franz, M.L., eds. (1988) *Studies in Jungian Psychology by Jungian Analysts: The Mother. Archetypal Image in Fairy Tales*. Toronto: Inner City Books. (Translated from German.)

Blake, K. (1977) The Sea-Dream: Peter Pan and Treasure Island. In *Annual of the Modern Language Association Division on Children's Literature and Children's Literature Association: Children's Literature, vol. 6*. New Haven: Yale University Press. pp. 165–181.

Blum, J. (1991) Ja-nej generationen vil have kontante svar. *Computerworld* (April).

Brøndsted, G.K. (1965) *Havfruens Saga. En litterar kunsthistorisk orientering ved Georg K. Brøndsted*. Copenhagen: C.E.C. Gads.

Broström, T. (1987) *Folkeeventyrets moderne genbrug eller hvad forfatteren gør*. Copenhagen: Gyldendal.

Brudal, J.P. (1984) *Det Ubevisste Språket. Psykologi og Symbolbilder i Folkeeventyrene*. Oslo: Universitetsforlaget.

Brun, B. (1989) Det evige flyvende barn. *Politiken* (12 marts). (Kronik.)

Brun, B. (1992) Alienation in Relation to the Instinct of Selfpreservation, Intellectual Drives and Libidinous Drives. A Psychodynamic Perspective. *Jahrbuch für Internationale Germanistik*. Reihe, A. Kongressberichte, band 29. Bern. pp.29–58.

Brun, B. and Skovgaard, B. (1983) Pinocchio et psykodrama. *Politiken* (9 marts). (Kronik.)

Campbell, J. (1972) Folkloristic Commentary. In J. Grimm and W. Grimm *The Complete Grimm's Fairytales*. New York: Random House.

Campbell, J. (1988). *Mythology/Philosophy: The Power of Myth*. New York: Doubleday. (Author interviewed by Bill Moyers.)

Christensen, S. (1976). *Tornerose i eventyrskoven og andre kapitler om folkeeventyr*. Copenhagen: Gyldendal.

Collodi, C. (1920) *Pinocchio*. New York: Lippincott.

Cooper, J.C. (1984) *Fairy Tales: Allegories of the Inner Life. Archetypal Patterns and Symbols in Classic Fairy Stories.* Wellingborough, Northampton: The Aquarian Press.

Cox, M. and Theilgaard, A. (1987) *Mutative Metaphors in Psychotherapy. The Aeolian Mode.* London: Tavistock Publications.

Dillistone, F.W. (1986) *The Power of Symbols.* London: SCM Press.

Dundes, A. (ed.)(1982) *Cinderella: A Folklore Casebook.* New York: Garland Publishing.

Erikson, E. (1968) *Identity, Youth and Crisis.* New York: W.W. Norton.

Fraiberg, S. (1973) *De magiskeår.* Copenhagen: Hans Reitzel. (Translated from *The Magic Years.*)

Fraser, M. (1976) *The Death of Narcissus.* London: Secker and Warburg.

Fromm, E. (1951) *Det Glemte Sprog.* Copenhagen: Hans Reitzel. (Translated from English: *The Forgotten Language.*)

Gay, P. (1988) *A Life for our Time.* New York: W.W. Norton.

Goldstein, J., Freud, A. and Solnit, A.J. (1973). *Beyond the Best Interests of the Child.* New York: Free Press.

Griffith, J. (1979) Making Wishes Innocent: Peter Pan. *The Lion and the Unicorn 3,* 28–37.

Grimm, J. and Grimm, W. (1972) *The Complete Grimm's Fairy Tales.* New York: Random House.

Grotstein, J.S. (1982) The Analysis of a Borderline Patient. In P. Giovacchini and L.B. Boyer (eds.) *Technical Factors in the Treatment of the Severely Disturbed Patient.* New York: Jason Aronson. pp.261–288.

Hallman, R.J. (1969) The Archetypes In Peter Pan. *Journal of Analytical Psychology 14,* 65–73.

Hark, H. (ed.) (1988) *Lexikon Jungscher Grundbegriffe.* Olten: Walter Verlag.

Heuscher, J.E. (1967) Death in the Fairy-Tale. *Diseases of the Nervous System 28,* 462–468.

Heuscher, J.E. (1974) *Myths and Fairy Tales. Their Origin, Meaning And Usefulness. A Psychiatric Study of Fairy Tales, 2nd ed.* Springfield. Illinois: Charles C. Thomas.

Hillman, J. (1988) *Archetypal Psychology.* Dallas, Texas: Spring Publications. (Originally published in 1981 as 'Psicologia Archetipica' in *Enciclopedia del Novecento,* Volume V.)

Hirsch, M. and Hirsch-Löwer, M. (1986) Ein Märchen vom ü bergangsobjekt. *Psyche 11,* 1025–1033.

Holbek, B. (1987) *Interpretation of Fairy Tales. Danish Folklore in a European Perspective.* Helsinki: Suomalainen Tiedeakatemia Academia Scientiarum Fennica.

Holbeck, B. (1991) Personal correspondence to Birgitte Brun.

Hubback, J. (1990) The Changing Person and the Unchanging Archetype. *Journal of Analytical Psychology 35,* 111–123.

Jørgensen, E.O. (1991) *Sct. Hans Hospital 1816–1991.* Roskilde: Sct. Hans Hospital.

Jellouschek, H. (1985) *Der Froschkönig.* Zürich: Kreuz Verlag.

Jung, C.G. (1956) *Symbols of Transformation. Collected works.* London: Routledge and Kegan Paul.

Karpe, M. (1956) The Origins of Peter Pan. *Psychoanalytic Review 43,* 104–110.

Kast, V. (1983) *Mann und Frau im Märchen.* Olten: Walter-Verlag.

Kast, V. (1989). *Märchen als Therapie.* München: Deutscher Taschenbuch Verlag.

Kaufmann, F. (1985) *Der Gestiefelte Kater.* Zürich: Kreuz Verlag.

Killingmo, B. (1990) Beyond Semantics: A Clinical and Theoretical Study of Isolation. *International Journal of Psycho-Analysis 71,* 113–126.

Lindgren, A. (1984) *The Robber's Daughter.* London: Methuen Children's Books. (Translated from Swedish.)

Lundgren, M. and Norrby, L.B. (1988) *Eventyrets helbredende kraft.* Copenhagen: Hans Reitzels. (Translated from Swedish.)

McCully, R.S. (1971) *Rorschach Theory and Symbolism.* Baltimore: Williams and Wilkins.

McDonald, M. (1974) Little Black Sambo. *Psychoanalytical Study of the Child 29,* 511–528.

Meisel, F.L. (1977) The Myth of Peter Pan. *Psychoanalytical Study of the Child 32,* 545–563.

Mudd, P. (1990) The Dark Self: Death As A Transferential Factor. *Journal of Analytical Psychology 35,* 125–141.

Müller, L. (1985) *Das Tapfere Schneiderlein.* Zürich: Kreuz Verlag.

Neilsen, T.I. (1986) *Bevidstheden og det som er helt anderledes.* Copenhagen Universitet: Psykologisk Laboratorium.

Neumann, E. (1974) *Bollingen Series, 47: The Great Mother. An Analysis of the Archetype.* Princeton, N.J.: Princeton University Press.

Neumann, E. (1976) *The Child, Structure and Dynamics of the Nascent Personality.* New York: Harper and Row.

Niederland, W.G. (1962) *A Psychoanalytic Inquiry into the Life and Work of Heinrich Schliemann. A Contribution to the Psychology of Genius.* Not published. 1–23.

Nielsen, M. (1983) *Salkvinden.* Copenhagen: Mallings.

Nielsen, T.I., Fensbo, U., Handberg, L., Hansen, K.W., Harkamp, M., Jensen, H.G., Kuhle, K., Laursen, E.K., Marner, L., Rasmus-Nielsen, B. and Rubin, J. (1983) *Fantasirejser. Veje til erkendelse af virkelighedens helhed og mangfoldighed.* Viborg: Klitrose.

Nyborg, E. (1962) *Den indre linie i H.C. Andersens eventyr. En psykologisk studie.* Copenhagen: Gyldendal.

Plato (1969) The Symposium. In *Collected Dialogue.* Princeton University Press.

Reisby, N. and Skogemann, P. (1985) *Karolines Bog.* Copenhagen: Rosinante.

Roheim, G. (1985) Aus dem Archiv der Psychoanalyse. Pinocchio. *Psyche 39,* 62–68.

Rose, J. (1984) *Language, Discourse, Society: The Case Of Peter Pan or The Impossibility of Children's Fiction.* London: Macmillan.

Scharfenberg, J. and Kämpfer, H. (1980) *Mit Symbolen Leben.* Olten: Walter Verlag.

Schneider, J. (1984) *Stress, Loss and Grief.* Baltimore: University Park Press.

Smith, B.L. (1990). Potential Space and the Rorschach: An Application of Object Relations Theory. *Journal of Personality Assessment 55,* 756–767.

Thompson, S. (1955–1958) *Motif-Index of Folkliterature.* Copenhagen: Rosenhilde og Bagger.

Thomsen, C.B.T. (1990) *Hitchcock hans liv og film.* Copenhagen: Gyldendal.

Trevarthen, C. (1975) Early Attempts at Speech. In R. Lewin (ed.) *Child Alive.* New York: Anchor Books.

Van Eenwyk, J.R. (1991) Archetypes: The strange attractors of the psyche. *Journal of Analytic Psychology 36,* 1–27.

von Franz, M.L. (1987) *Interpretation of Fairy Tales.* Dallas, Texas: Spring Publications. (Translated from German)

von Franz, M.L. (1989) *Eventyrfortolkning. En Introduktion.* Copenhagen: Gyldendal.

Wallerstein, R.S. (1989) The Psychotherapy Research Project of the Menninger Foundation: An Overview. *Journal of Consulting Clinical Psychology 57,* 195–205.

Wharton, B. (1990) The Hidden Face of Shame: The Shadow, Shame and Separation. *Journal of Analytical Psychology 35,* 279–299.

Winnicott, D. (1975) Transitional Objects and Transitional Phenomena. In *Through Paediatrics to Psychoanalysis*. New York: Basic Books.

Wivel, O. (1961) *Templet for Kybele*. Copenhagen: Gyldendal.

Wöller, H. (1984) *Aschenputtel*. Zürich: Kreuz Verlag.

Zeiler, J. (1986) Marc Chagall – Ansätze zu einer Psychobiographie. *Psyche*, 1123–1148.

Zielen, V. (1987) *Hans im Glück*. Zürich: Kreuz Verlag.

Suggested Reading

Bodkin, M. (1965). *Archetypal Patterns in Poetry, Psychological Studies of Imagination*, London: Oxford University Press.

Brun, G., and Brun, G. (1946). A Psychological Treatise On Hans Andersen's Fairy Tale 'Thumbelina'. *Acta Psycht. et. Neurol.* 21, 141-149.

Bührmann, V. M. (1987). The Feminine in Witchcraft: Part 2. *Journal of Analytical Psychology* 32, 257-277.

Clinton, J. W. (1986). Madness and Cure in the Thousand and One Nights. In *Fairy Tales and Society: Illusion, Allusion and Paradigm*, R. B. Bottigheimer, ed. Philadelphia: University of Pennsylvania Press, pp.36-51.

Drewermann, E., and Neuhaus, I. (1984) *Grimms Mrchen tiefenpsychologisch gedeutet: Schneeweisschen und Rosenrot*, 2nd ed. Olten und Freiburg in Breisgau: Walter.

Eifermann, R. R. (1987) Fairy Tales – a Royal Road to the Child Within the Adult. *Scand. Psychoanal. Rev.* 10, 51-77.

Eimer, K. W. (1989) 'The Assessment and Treatment of the Religiously Concerned Psychiatric Patient.' *The Journal of Pastoral Care* XLIII.3 231-241.

Erickson, R. C. (1990) 'Serving the Needs of Persons With Chronic Mental Illness: A Neglected Ministry.' *The Journal of Pastoral Care* XLIV.2 153-162.

Hjortsø, L. (1971) *Grske Guder og Helte*, Copenhagen: Politikens Forlag.

Holbek, B. (1989) *Tolkning af Trylleeventyr*, Copenhagen: Nyt Nordisk Forlag, Arnold Busck.

Holbek, B., and Pi, I. (1967) *Fabeldyr og Sagnfolk*. Copenhagen: Politikens Forlag.

Lotz, M. (1988) *Eventyrbroen. Psykoanalytiske essays om H. C. Andersen*, Copenhagen: Gyldendal.

Lubetsky, M. J. (1989) The Magic of Fairy Tales: Psychodynamic and Developmental Perspectives. *Child Psychiatry and Human Development* 19, 245-255.

Lykke, N. (1989) *Skriftserie fra Center for Kvindestudier, 3: Rdtte og dipus. Brikker til en feministisk psykoanalyse*, Odense: Odense Universitetsforlag.

Moyer, F. S. (1989) 'Pastoral Care in the Hospital' *The Journal of Pastoral Care* XLIII.2 171-183.

Pruyser, P. W. (1984) 'Religion in the Psychiatric Hospital: A Reassessment.' *The Journal of Pastoral Care* XXXVIII.1 5-16.

Vedfelt, O. (1990) *Drmenes Dimensioner. Drmenes vsen, funktion og fortolkning*. Copenhagen: Gyldendals Bogklubber.

Whitlock, G. E. (1990) 'Change in Faith Experiences and in Psychotherapy.' *Journal of Pastoral Care* XLIV.2 173-181.

Subject Index

achievement drives 7, 29
active imagination 39
Aeolian Mode of dynamic
    psychotherapy 10
age, psychological 30–1
'an as-if personality' 15–16
analogue ways of thinking
    17–18
androgynous
    characteristics, Peter
    Pan's 86, 87, 88–9
angel symbols 15, 126
animal body symbols 122–3
animal fantasies 45, 118–19
animal symbols 122
'apple symbols 11
archetypes 5, 7, 52–3, 93, 94,
    121, 123–4

babies, symbol formation 8
baldness symbols 126
ball symbols 126
bear symbols 123
beard symbols 94
Bible
    New Testament 71, 74, 77,
        80, 81
    Old Testament 73, 77, 89
bipolarity of archetypes 5
    see also good-evil
        contrasts
bird symbols 14–15, 87, 98,
    101, 123
birth themes 87, 88, 111, 123
black paint symbol 109–10
blood symbols 123
bodily contact fantasies 97–8
Briar Rose 57–8, 69–70

Captain Hook, in *Peter Pan*
    85, 90–1
Cat with the Boots, The 70
chaplaincy, in psychiatric
    hospitals 63–4, 65
child development 8, 24,
    30–1, 35, 79–80

physically ill example
    26–7
    see also emotionally
        deprived children
child symbols 86, 98
Cinderella 10, 40, 57–8, 76–7,
    121–2
coffin symbols 126
collective unconsious 121
comfort, fairy tales as 64, 66,
    67, 79–80
conflict, identification
    through fairy tales
    28–9, 57, 65, 67–8, 78
contamination 118
continuity needs,
    emotionally disturbed
    children 47–8
contraction principle 10
conversations, fairy tale 2,
    27, 63–81
    choosing 77–8
    material used 67–77
    narrative method 66–7
Corinthians, Ist Letter to the
    74
creating fairy tales 34, 43–5,
    56, 58–61
crisis intervention, through
    fairy tales 32
cultural symbols 122, 126–8

Darling, Mr, in *Peter Pan* 89,
    91, 101
death of an archetypal
    figure 123–4
death themes 5, 86, 87, 123
'delinquent teenager'
    fantasy example 24
development, child 8, 24,
    30–1, 35, 79–80
'developmental conflict'
    type fairy tales 78
    *see also Briar Rose, Cat
        with the Boots, Peter
        Pan, Snow White*
*Devil with the Three Golden
    Hairs, The* 55
diagnostic power of fairy
    tales 28, 29
diamond symbols 61
digital ways of thinking 17
dog symbols 124

doll symbols 126
dove symbols 87
dragon symbols 29, 125
drawings *see* illustrations
drives (instincts) 7, 29
dualism 25
    see also good-evil
        contrasts

earth symbols 124
egg symbols 26, 98
emotional contact, through
    fairy tales 24, 29
emotionally deprived
    children 2, 25–6, 40,
    43, 47–61
    creating own tales 58–61
    early memories 49–50
    fantasy and reality 50–1
    guidance through fairy tales
    54–8
    mother-images 52–4
    symbols in fairy tales 51–2
'eternal child' symbol 86
everyday life, symbols in
    11–13
evil-good contrasts 10, 25,
    52–3, 89
Evil Mother images 52–3, 61
    see also stepmothers;
        witches
externalisation 9

'failure' type fairy tales 78
    *see also Hans in Luck;
        Valiant Little Tailor*
fairy symbols 29, 125–6
    in *Peter Pan* 91, 99
Fairy Tale Wood, The 59–61
fairy tales, classification and
    definition 18–19
fantasy-reality distinction
    24, 35, 49, 50–1
father images 11, 37, 55, 61,
    72
    in *Peter Pan* 85, 89, 90–1,
        96, 101
    in *Pinocchio* 55, 91, 106,
        114–15
feather symbols 124
Fisherman and His Wife, The
    70–1
fisherman symbols 126

Author Index